CW00971419

Complexity, Death, and Nothing

Complexity, Death, and Nothing

Jason Edwards

Luminous
Patch
Press

2016

Complexity, Death, and Nothing
© Jason Edwards/Luminous Patch Press, 2016

All rights reserved. No part of this publication may be reproduced, stored in a retrieval system, or transmitted, in any form, or by any means, electronic, mechanical, photocopying, recording or otherwise, without the prior written permission of the publishers.

Jason Edwards has asserted his right under the Copyright, Designs and Patents Act, 1988, to be identified as author of this work.

British Library Cataloguing-in-Publication Data
A catalogue record for this book is available from the British Library.

Cover image: L.L. Fitzgerald, *From An Upstairs Window, Winter* (National Gallery of Canada)
Image on page 92: Roman Reisinger, *Still Life With Lanterns and Shells* (Galerie Roman Reisinger)

Contents

In every language the loveliest question
Is, You can say that?

Eve Kosofsky Sedgwick

I

A Different Person

A Different Person

Being in your voice
Feels like being held, or home,
Sweetly maddening.

♦

Virginal, humble
As a hope, a horse's head,
Up against your hand.

The willingness of
The beads to be numbered and
Touched, proud and mindful.

(Tacit: "I would like
To see you barefoot, to rub
You down with oil, salt").

♦

Your hand next to mine,
Second time at the Habit,
You speculate that

A mise-en-abyme
For Merrill's writing could be
Two male lovers' hands

Open to others'
Voices, moving a single
Chinese, ouija cup.

♦

Civil partnership
Fills the papers. I'm so bored.
Yet I draft this text:

"Can we get married,
Raise this cat, a brood of kids,
A big, happy dog?"

If we were partnered,
And I were to take your name,
I'd become 'J.M.'

♦

Not wanting to stop,
Find I lack Dr. Detre's
Flair for the last word.

II

1441

1: Blurb

A man leaves a man, and a world turns on
Its end. The man, then, meets another man
With a similar name. At the same time,
Our protagonist starts a relation
With his first transactional analyst:
It's meant to help him make the transition.
A comic blend of insight and blindness,
Their meetings gradually change everything.
All of this while, watching him from the wings,
A group of key friends. A sort of half-assed
Sonnet sequence in which the poet turns
Forty, and tries to account for himself,
Be warned: these poems are melancholic
And also joyfully pornographic.

2: Title Poem

I'd long wanted call this collection,
1441, a queer obsession.
I quite liked the modernist concision:
The number of lines found in a sonnet
Juxtaposed with the age of the poet;
Admired the palendromic character.
But it was only when Victoria
Started browsing on Wikipedia,
For key events that happened in that year,
That the real appeal finally came clear:
King's Cambridge, where I spent my sore twenties,
Was first founded in the 1440s.
You can take the boy out of the college;
Unrecognised, pain will do you damage.

3: Cover Image

A cold December day in South London,
We're at the Dulwich picture gallery,
The exhibition that's on: Tom Thompson
And the Group of Seven, Canadian
Landscape painting from the last century.
Punch drunk with events from the night before,
The fight we had at his birthday party
Would frieze me out of his life completely.
But, for now, he is showing me around
The new environment he left me for:
Outside, frost on the trees, snow on the ground,
Inside, more similarly polar scenes
That have always felt most like home to me;
One of these, the cover image, surely.

4: Dedication: For Eve Kosofsky Sedgwick, in Memory.

I did not know back then what today meant:
The last time Eve and I saw each other.
The sound of voices, slow walk to the door,
Greetings and ice tea in her apartment.
Unloading my rucksack, both she and Hal
Amazed I could travel with so little.
Awkward, as always, at the beginning.
Ambling gently, in the November sun,
To lunch, one block north: an invalid pace.
A child unable to let anyone
Be kind to him, I paid the bill myself.
Eve was disappointed, but patient that
I could not yet learn the lesson of her
Generosity and her indolence.

5: Separate Beds

We woke up, the day that I turned forty,
As we had done, more often than we'd not,
In separate beds, in separate rooms.
We'd started off together hours before,
But I had a pretty serious cough,
And though he thought that I was faking it,
It had stopped him from sleeping, and so he
Had left me in the middle of the night.
I don't think that we ever shared again
A bed, though we made out for the last time,
Tenderly, the day after my birthday.
In the sea, I held him with all my heart,
The last peaceful moment that we would share
Before so many brutal, ugly fights.

6: Bad Karma

How much hurt there was between us back then,
Corrosive pain that kept interrupting
The equally heart-felt acts of kindness:
His need to make me pay for my birthday
Meaning that I simply couldn't take in
The love that saw a bowl in the market
And knew that it was just perfect for me.
Sitting having dessert that afternoon,
I needed to talk about everything,
Whilst he preferred the sweetness of silence.
He nearly broke the plate as he stormed out.
I couldn't stop shaking on the way home.
He was out cold whilst I watched the TV,
With so much history, we couldn't be.

7: First and Last

The first time I that saw you on campus,
With Lawrence, "Gosh, handsome" is what I thought.
When my then-boyfriend and I began to
Have an open relationship, the first
Thing that came into my mind was "Maybe
I could have sex with that graduate boy".
For months, this year, you would be the first thing
On my mind at the start of each long day,
When the cat and I both woke up purring
In the sunshine; the last thing on my mind
As I would count up my blessings at night,
Under my hot quilt, with my feet left out.
If I see you again, "Little has changed"
Is probably the last thing I should say.

8: Hindsight

I wasn't very kind to you when we
First met. I made some facetious remark
About how many Bens there were in the
Department and how I couldn't keep them
Separate in my mind. How that comment
Came back to bite me, was more revealing
Than I knew. What I did not know, then, was
That my boyfriend had already left me.
He'd just not let me know; and you would break
My heart the following summer. The first
Omens were there, though: that day you saw me
Cruising you from a distance, on campus;
Returning for a closer look, you came
Back, adjusted your rucksack, then went home.

9: Goodbye

Remember the day he moved to London?
The drive to the capital's yelling hell?
Eating fast food at the service station?
The raid on the shop below his new flat?
Was it lost on him, it seemed to be, that
His new housemate was a version of me?
An older man with a Cambridge degree.
We could have been direct peers, it turned out,
Though we didn't have a single person
In common, except, perhaps, now for him.
Buying some food in the supermarket,
I could not cry, I was feeling so sad.
"I can't believe you're not staying with me"
He said, as I left him, perhaps for good.

10: Your Tongue, Like the Sun, in My Mouth

"According to his housemate, he blows hot
And cold": It's clear that Clare is warning me.
But the reason I've come to this party
Is solely in the hope of seeing you.
I'd spotted on Facebook that you might come,
So I watch the door, talk to Carolyn,
For an hour, trying not to look restless.
I'm sure it's shamefully conspicuous.
Earlier that summer, I had woken
Up in a single, Bristol hotel bed.
Rather, so hot for you I could not sleep,
Came at the thought of your tongue in my mouth.
In total, you'd send me thousands of texts;
You'd drop conversations without a thought.

11: Solstice

We drive to the beach, have a flask of tea,
Walk in the mild ozone on Christmas Day.
Before New Year, I nearly get knocked down,
Going home. I call on Victoria.
I can't stop crying. She advises me
"You can't be falling down any more stairs.
You have to leave him before things get worse".
I phone him at home, gave him the sad news.
In June, months again ahead, when she said
"Jason, please put him down and walk away.
Hold your pain like you're holding a baby".
(Me, an infant who had never been held).
How much of my suffering she's witnessed;
How much more she has kindly prevented.

12: Boundaries

At the agreed time, Tuesdays and Thursdays,
I'm slowly but surely working out her
Boundaries. I'm to arrive there promptly.
Should use the knocker. After initial
Greeting, there's to be no talking on the
Stairs. I'm to follow her up quietly.
At the end of the session, I'm to see
Myself out the door. No email's allowed.
I'm to phone her. Otherwise, "we will cheat
Ourselves of the experience", she says.
If I do all this, will it feel less like
Going through motions and more like a life?
Will my heavy heart start feeling lighter?
Will I stop feeling sick all of the time?

13: Spring

Although I have never understood why,
I have always liked that Wilfred Owen
Poem in which the reader is asked to
Move a dying soldier into the sun.
And then it came clear, like ice sloughed off a
Roof in a midday, February thaw.
"I think you thought", she said to me one day,
"That being in therapy would be like
Taking your sculpture and moving it to
A different environment, one where there
Was more warmth and light. But our process here's
To melt down your statue, to bring you back
To life". I could have cried with relief. "No
More trenches, no mere survival, you say?"

14: Asshole

I wonder, to what extent does it start
Here and now? On Valentine's Day, he and
I going to a poetry reading.
I feel afraid: he cannot stop texting.
He tells me about how his friend kissed you.
"I did not know that they knew each other..."
"Yes", he replies, "from chatting on Grindr".
I learn that you call yourself an asshole;
That you, drunkenly, kiss the friend goodnight.
I think, at the time, I should ask you out.
If you've kissed him, you might surely want me.
If you say that to me, I think later,
I will reply "how there's lots of fun things
You can do with an asshole", one so sweet.

15: Together

That weekend, how quickly it came undone.
I get out the bath, come in to see him,
Lay down next to him, my head on his chest.
He does not quite recoil, but I suspect
He isn't feeling fully comfortable.
"Is that ok?" I ask. "Depends", he says.
"I think it blurs things". I withdraw again,
And ask him "Are you seeing someone else?"
"Yes", he replies. The world stops spinning then,
Throws me clean off, out into cold, deep space.
I wonder, did he notice we both kept
Singing, those last three days, a Patrick Wolf
Refrain: "I can do this alone, but we
Can do this so much better, together"?

16: Habit Forming

On the night that we went on our first date,
I felt abashed about using your name,
So, to my friends, I referred to you as
"The Cult of [your full name]". I changed my sheets,
Took a bath, tidied from top to bottom.
We sat by the door, and the Habit was
So cold each time someone arrived, you could
See your breath. If I was nervous, you were
Probably scared to death; awkward for sure.
I had prepared questions, you, your answers.
We were the last to leave, were there for hours.
An awkward goodbye where I think you would
Have kissed someone else. I sent you a text:
"Thanks for a lovely time. More soon, sweet dreams".

17: Don't Fall in Love

If you're a middle child, to whom the world
Seems like a Malthusian place, with too
Little space, ever scarcer resources,
Your care a precious, rare commodity,
Don't set your heart on a loved only child:
He'll take your gifts for granted; not his fault -
He's used to being adored, to a world
That revolves around him, rotates under
His feet; won't notice if he disappears
From your life for a week, will expect you
To show up when he needs your help. This sense
Of entitlement is his birthright, just
The way it's always been. Don't fall for him?
That I want him's a symptom, not a whim.

18: Safe Sex Sonnet

"Jason", you warn me, "I'm just not feeling
Very sex positive at the moment.
Anal sex hurts, whatever people say,
Even if it's preceded by rimming".
Empathetic, sympathetic, turned on,
I want to appear cosmopolitan:
"Yes, however many poppers one takes".
As if I've ingested alkyl nitrite.
I've told myself, I'm paid to use my brain,
I can't afford to keep fucking with it,
Even for the sake of a gentler lay.
Smiling, sharing, I look you in the eye,
And I say, "Nothing's better than kissing,
There is nothing that is more intimate".

19: Dropped

It took courage, ok some of it Dutch,
For me to ask, at the very end of
Our eight-hour second date, if we could fix
Up our next meet before we said goodbye.
"It's just that I am not very good at
The start of relationships, I find them
Crazy making". You're just ahead of me,
Stumbling towards the stairs: "Right back at you".
A week later, when we're due to go out,
Back for another drink at the Habit,
You cancel in the morning, claiming work.
You go on a campus bar crawl instead.
One true word's gonna beat a pack of lies;
Won't be the last time I'll feel dropped inside.

20: Ordinary

You tell me you have written something new,
An ordinary piece on Eliot.
So I propose some tea and cake to you.
Friday at Betty's? We arrange to meet.
I couldn't love being in your voice more,
It's as intimate as we'll ever get.
We talk, it's a little awkward. The first
Time we've met sober, it's a lot briefer.
I'm a pretty brutal critic. You say
You don't mind, that it's all grist to the mill
Of your narcissism. I think that what
We make together is better than what
We separately fashion. I get home,
You're already on Grindr. I'm alone.

21: Trilobite

In the Spring, I wondered if I could buy
A temporary tattoo, somewhere online,
That was made according to my design:
A trilobite was what I had in mind.
Hardy describes a scene where a man falls
Off a cliff, and eyes up such a fossil.
What then unfolds? A geological
Pre-history of the entire region.
My shrink must have seen the markings on my
Arm, that day, considered what it might mean.
Time passed. It would come clear when V. compared
My unearthing you, some six months later,
To famished squirrels digging in the ground,
For nuts buried earlier that winter.

22: Sense and Insincerity

"I'd like to accept your invitation
To dinner", you write to me, "but I just
Wanted to check that we are meeting on
A platonic basis". You say you fear
To ask this, you then pause, since I have not
Given you any clear indication
That I am attracted to you. You sense
That, in posing this, you might cause offense.
It's just that you "thrive on clear boundaries,
Are not romantically available
At the moment". I cry inside; reply
Immediately, thanking you for your
Message, say that it's "helpful, kind, and clear".
Denying my love would be insincere.

23: Cold Feet

You are drenched when you arrive for dinner,
Two days later. In the narrow hall, I
Invite you in, negotiate your bike.
You are afraid that you'll mess up my space.
I lead you through into the living room,
Immaculate, and beautifully lit.
I offer to take your coat, hang it on
The newel-post to air. I see your shoes,
Socks and feet must be completely wet through.
I am not sure what I can do. I can't
Say out loud "Might I unlace those for you,
Towel your ankles and soles gently dry?"
You can't relax or sit still, pace the floor,
Lean nervously on the radiator.

24: Second Portion

In the kitchen, I open a bottle
Of red wine and prepare Indian food.
When it's done, I serve you first, then myself.
We go back through, I put on some music,
Sit down next to you, the cat helpfully
Asleep in the only other nearby
Chair. We have a second portion. On the
TV, a photo of my family.
We talk about your ma and pa, desire
For a big bunch of kids. I explain that
I am mostly against gay marriage, but
How sometimes you just meet someone you love.
You concur. Later, you should go, you think,
I say "no need, let's have another drink".

25: Ironic

"Ok", you say, "can I use your bathroom?"
"Of course", I reply, "turn left at the top
Of the stairs, and just keep going; the light
Switch is immediately on the right".
You take a piss. I can hear this, since I
Live in an Edwardian terrace. What
I don't hear is that you fart. When I go
Up to the loo myself, I notice there
That you must have found the air freshener.
You perhaps felt mortified that I would
Judge this shameful infant scene, but I find
That I love this thoughtful, awkward young man
More than the ironic facade online.

26: Gym Buddy

For a while, on Monday nights and Thursdays
You'd text me from the gym, conversations
That would last for up to two or three hours.
I'd be lying in the bath, on a chair.
Rhythms unpredictable, insistent,
Would characterise the to and the fro.
You'd send me songs, musical theatre
Hyperlinks; I'd reciprocate in kind.
We'd both be clever, laughing, all the while.
At some point, you would take a shower, there
Would be a pause and then you would return,
Fully dressed and ready to go, whilst I'd
Have made tea in the meantime. You'd get home,
I'd prep for bed, you in my heart and head.

27: Brunch Date

Previously, when you'd talked of your beau,
Your paramour, it had felt like we were
Sharing something, had broken a taboo;
We had begun to become intimate.
At brunch, you are talking in comic tones
About your broken heart, a boy you knew,
Who'd come, last summer, on to my boyfriend.
My heart hurts. In fact, I'm so punch drunk you
Are forced to pay the bill on the way out.
You're half an hour late to our last lunch date,
Claim, at your's, there's a queue for the shower.
When you arrive, with your cycle helmet
But not your glasses, you're willow patterned
From the night before. Still I wait, adore.

28: He Changes His Profile Picture

From afar, you tell me about waking
Up hard next to a straight friend, spooning him.
You get me confessional, excited.
"I love you", I say more or less out loud.
Later, when I look you up on Facebook,
I find you have changed your profile picture.
You've replaced the lovely shot of you in
An Australian gallery, wearing
No socks, looking up at Jacob's Ladder,
With a severe, magisterial and
Austere new black and white photo, in which
Your friend appears, a dream above your head.
Later that week, too busy to see me,
The same friend is, again, close to your bed.

29: Ring

I awoke this morning and my heart sank
Heavy in my chest. I wanted to text.
But to what end? To say, can we stand close
So I can rest my head upon your chest?
Bony hip on hip, look up to your face?
(A maternal embrace). With a slow blink,
Tell you I have missed you this last, wet week?
"Bit of a cliché?" I fear you respond.
Then how about this? I have filed my nails
With the gathering folds of your anus
In mind; hope to feel the tight compression
Of your warm, soft and clammy bowel wall
Around my finger; as I press upon
The walnut inside you, to feel you smile.

30: Sext

You text me from the G.U.M. clinic,
Scared, and tell me how the condom had broke,
That though he had not ejaculated
In you, he'd also slipped you inside him.
(Everything would turn out to be alright
For you both). "I am not phobic about
Bug chasing", I say, "I have read Tim Dean,
But you are very precious to me; please
Don't take risks with yourself". Punctilious,
As ever, you correct me: "It was booze,
Not bug chasing". I tell you how painful
It is for me to get, by text, this news.
"Could any part of you ever want me?"
"I don't think that's feasible", you reply.

31: Later, That Same Afternoon

"Do I need you out of touch for a while?"
"I don't know, I need to think about that.
Give me time". There is a pause. "I am not
All that", you say. I exhale and send you
Another poem which, undefended,
Can only do us both more harm than good.
"It might be a cruel thing to say, but
Your loving me has really helped me see
That not everyone who likes me's crazy."
Cruel is not the word; that loving you has
Somehow helped someone be closer to you
Than I will ever be allowed to be?
Getting home, I lie down, and start to cry.
Still I find that I cannot say goodbye.

32: In Which I Don't Yet Know He Is Saying Goodbye

I spend the morning sorting out the house,
Filing papers, polishing surfaces,
Washing the floors, and rinsing out the cloths.
I also take a bath. You arrive late,
As you most often do. You are wearing
A cycle helmet that you've taken off
By the time you knock on the door. I see
Now that you have both started taking care
Of yourself - you have internalised me,
At least to this degree - and paused to make
Sure that your hair, which you know I admire,
Looks as good as it can possibly be.
I make you lunch; you read me your paper.
After that, for three months, you disappear.

33: In His Idiom

If we do ever finally make love,
I'd like it to be almost entirely
In your idiom: lying in your bed,
Under your duvet, embraced in your scent,
Dewed in your fresh sweat; missionary, yes,
At first; enough space in your mind to be
Remembering me. I know already
That we share some things. For instance, we might
Want to light incense, one smell in the air
Could be Nag Champa: rising wisps of smoke,
Ash dropping silent on your windowsill,
A mantle somewhere. Both default bottoms,
In the abstract, bringing together our
Previous scripts will ensure that it is

34: Hard for Me

Unpredictable, spontaneously
Flexible, as we discover what we
Can make together. Speaking for myself
Personally, I'm imagining that
We'll be a bit drunk, playful and sincere,
Giddy, funny, and sober. Finally,
You'll grow quiet and soft, hard for you as me;
Will help me to talk to you without words,
Making eye contact, by moving, reaching,
Breathing and feeling. I'll be curious
To find out what your feet look like, to feel
The deep ache of long, lovely you pushing
Gently into me, uncomfortably,
Tentatively and necessarily

35: Umbilical

Forcibly, at first, then more rhythmically,
Unselfconsciously, coming inside me.
Staying there, and taller than me by a
Considerable degree, you'd surround
Me fully, your sweaty palm and fingers
Wrapped around mine indistinguishably.
Softening inside, filling me up, we'd
Be foetal, contained, calm and still, like twins,
Floating in warm, amniotic fluid.
I would not stop you from separating
From me when you are finally ready;
But, for now, intermittently clenching
My sphincter, I lovingly hold you back,
Aware of all the parts of you I lack.

36: Opening Up

"Don't see anyone you don't already
Know", she instructs me. "Don't open up
Any new sources of pain". I concur.
Three weeks later, however, after a
Trans-Atlantic flight, my knees really hurt.
So I ask my then masseur if she might
Target the pain and try to unpick it.
She locates the aches, works at the marbles
In my shoulder blades and neck; then she gets
Down to my thighs. "Have you ever had a
Knee injury?" she asks. "Because your quads
Feel like they have never been anything
Other than tense." I tear up, cry inside;
Am once again shattered by the roadside.

37: August

I admit that sending you that poem
About rimming was probably ill-judged;
That I should have paid much more attention
Early on, when you told me that you thrived
On clear boundaries. It's just that when I
Got your last text in that July exchange,
My compassion for you was so alive,
I hoped that it might make you feel more loved.
If anything that I've since said or done
Has stopped you from wanting to be in touch,
To meet me for a drink, come round for lunch,
From sharing your ideas and needs with me,
From being face to face with me in my
Rocking chair or office, I am sorry.

38: Departure Lounge

Nothing has changed since the last time you came.
I still love you, only now it's tacit,
Hopeless, professional, from a distance.
I've had to adjust to the fact that there
Is a boyfriend now, that you have seem to have
Forgotten how to be in touch with me.
(I hope that he knows, how lucky is he).
Stopped using Twitter; unsubscribed from you
On Facebook. I just couldn't bare to read
Another reference to a hot boy
That you wanted in Denmark or elsewhere.
The worst moment was El Paso airport:
Six thousand miles, twenty-two hours from home,
I don't think I've ever felt so alone.

39: Preterition

I find that I keep saying to myself:
"I just don't understand, I don't know what
To do for the best." And how did I come
To be so fully repressed in your mind?
Such that you keep forgetting to reply,
Send apologies when I prompt you to,
Tell me how great it would be to see me,
But then just drop me again to the floor.
At first, five days pass; then three weeks. Later,
You notice the pause and pick up the thread.
In the meantime, I have been heartbroken.
But, of course, I do know what has happened,
What I have done: I told you I loved you,
And now that can't be taken back, undone.

40: The One Where They Meet on Campus

"I don't think that you could have hurt me more
If you had tried, in August", are some words
I am working hard not to say aloud.
Others would include: "I really miss you".
"Why haven't you been in touch for six weeks?"
You're so uncertain and ashamed, you fear
That I won't acknowledge you, stop or smile.
But I do, could not be happier to
See you. "Thanks for your message". (I talk first).
"I'd like to meet. Might you propose a date?"
So this is how I love you now: with my
Eyes closed, face stilled, and with fake composure.
Which part of "I love you" didn't you get?
It was good for life when I told you that.

41: Pattern

Walking to dinner, I realise how
Close I am coming to Gell's Farmhouse where
My ex lived when we first got together.
And when I ask A. who hurt him the most
Your name is the one he reaches for first.
Our stories are strikingly similar:
He couldn't resist your gaucheness either,
Made the fatal mistake of telling you
How much he liked you. Then you closed the door,
Never spoke to him again. This pattern
Would be heavy handed in a poem.
This does not make me love you one bit less.
Songs shuffle randomly in my ear-phones,
A bright, not quite full moon lights my way home.

42: Shrink

For a while now, I have been pondering
Who you obtained those diagnoses from?
Your narcissistic personality
Disorder, you warned me about, and I
Heard of your "terrifying maternal
Superego". I looked up the first one.
Not as good a description of you as
The fact that you're a total Gemini.
Feeling how devastating your no is,
I have been wondering about your mum:
Your boyfriend as an act of defiance?
The way that you ruthlessly used your ex
To show your parents that you had grown up;
To tell your housemate, you, too, could have sex.

43: Anniversary

If, a year ago, before he moved out,
He had said to me that we'd find ourselves,
In September, in this bright changing room,
Undressing again, quite self-consciously,
As on our famous, clinching swimming date -
When, seeing his blunt feet for the first time,
I stared, and he felt judged, and I could not
Yet say aloud "it's as if I've dreamt you" -
Or sunbathing on a scorching concrete
Rooftop, too hot for our poor soles; cruising
Together in an Indian summer;
I'd not have known whether to laugh or cry.
Truth be told, when I got back home today,
I still had no idea which to try.

44: Waiting to Exhale

The last time he was fully inside me,
Lying in bed, my feet above his head,
"I love fucking you, J", is what he said.
The art of exhaling to hold that part
Of him within: warm, hot, hard, uncertain.
Neither of us knew it, at that moment,
But this scene would never happen again.
I gave to Oxfam two of his brother's
Old jumpers, and his 'fifties bowling shirt.
I still wear his striped pyjama bottoms,
The after-shave bought for him by his mum.
His cast-off sheets feel like another skin.
Remembering this, happiness still comes
Surprisingly quick, like, well, [...] like come.

45: Here

Here is what I learned when he went away:
That music travels up to the room in
Which he used to lay, revealing to me
How much space I used to take up, how much
Of me he put up with. In the evenings,
I find that I'm restless, even if I
Watch TV or take a bath. I find he
Left behind the last Christmas gift I bought.
I've got mixed feelings about that. It's like
He's still with me even though he has gone.
If it's possible to be loved by friends,
There's hope. But these days it's enough to be
Heard when I show up with integrity,
However heartbroken that I may be.

46: Two Reasons (for Mel and Adam)

"There are two reasons", Adam says to me,
"Why he will never meet anyone else
As good as you are. Firstly, because of
Who he is. If he could not find a way
To use your love, to let it transform him,
What hope in hell does anyone else have?
And secondly, and more simply", he says,
With a boyish smile, "because there is no
One else in the world better than you are".
("I don't think I have ever loved you more":
The sentence that I hold inside of me).
I do not say anything in reply.
Looking for somewhere to buy sandwiches,
I grow quiet. We keep walking awhile.

47: Bluebeard in the Grindrvers

There was the one wanting to be pissed on;
The master's boy who showed up in my class;
North-west guy seeks double penetration,
Unsurprisingly, a pain in the ass;
Jon, who was an Oxford music student;
The lad kissing dolphins in a wet suit;
A New Haven Latin American.
Then there was the Allegory of Death;
Ben, his camera in the photograph;
The silent man who wrote and wrote and wrote,
Who'd already had a date with my ex.
Sometimes it feels like you're Henry the Eighth,
Sometimes like a decapitated wife.

48: Sandsend

"You are asking the wrong questions", she said,
As we sat on the sea wall at Sandsend.
It takes me a while, but I understand:
"Who he is doesn't matter?" I respond.
"You were looking for something specific",
She continued, "like a kind of seabird,
Trawling the shore". What comes to mind, I find:
Mollusk shrapnel, soft sea glass, weathered stones.
"Also, the timing seemed quite important.
In the session, Betsy had encouraged
You to stop talking to your ex- a while.
You agreed, then invited him straight out".
"It was like I hit Betsy on her head
With a crowbar; loved him, not her?" I said.

49: Shy

How and why did it take me half a life
To realise that I have two ways of
Being shy, both as counterproductive?
There is the introspective kind: the one
Where my face burns, heart hurts, and shoulders drop;
My voice loses its gravity and depth;
I feel afraid she's going to hit me,
Retaliate; humiliate; hurt me;
Where the air between us feels very thin.
Then there's the other kind, where she says I'm
Talking at her, or to her, rather than
With her; where I'm confident, extrovert,
Articulate, but can't make eye contact;
Look anywhere in the room but at her.

50: Performative (York)

More recently, I have found a new way
To be: I speak from my chest, more deeply,
Slowly, hesitantly; there are pauses,
Spaces, to think, reflect; to wait and find
Out what's happening inside me and in
Between us; where she gets to interrupt
Me, gets a word in edgewise; where I make
Simple sentences of the kind that I'm
Constantly encouraging my students,
In tutorials, to write; where there's an
"I" followed by a simple verb and noun.
It takes a while; but at the end of the
Session, I tell her, "I seem to like this.
Do you think that we can keep doing it?"

51: Technique

Hoping it might help my hurting soften,
Friday, early evening, I go walking,
Whilst I wait for Izzy to fix our date.
I think I see you twice, first on your bike,
Cycling past St John's. Then ahead of me,
A red puffer jacket, on Gillygate,
Reminds me of the uncertainty on
Your face as you came in on our first date.
Not sure how I can keep on letting go,
Each day, but I do. I know I miss you,
This week, when the butt plug comes in the post.
I open the packet, lubricate it,
Sit down, having stripped. I give, and it's in.
I comfort myself where you might have been.

52: Against Evidence (for Lauren)

J[…] describes the charm campaign you're waging,
R[-] reports that you are just a boy;
J[…] complains about your brusque arrogance,
Hurt, A[--] has never been less coy;
V[-] wonders if you are bipolar;
I[-] satirises your Facebook posts;
My worries, I share with E[---],
Who says "talk to A[-], and not L[-]".
"Maybe he is just the kind of person",
V[---] speculates, "who people
Fall in love with". B[-] smiles as she sees
My strategy. I still want you to be
In love with me. It makes no difference.
Precious details, not damning evidence.

53: Cairn (for Izzy)

Izzy writes to me and tells me about
Having her guitar professionally
Restrung; the only thing she has from home.
I consider what it must mean for her
To cradle it, to hold it in her arms.
I know how it feels, both to be homeless
And to be held by her: the sustained care
Needed to repair an abandonment.
These days, she is like the air that I breathe,
My backbone: the kind of thing you'd regret
If it wasn't there, so sure you forget
How, without it, you'd crumble, couldn't be.
She's the stone cairn my family built me
On my birthday whilst I swam in the sea.

54: #dumbass

I'd never been much good at this genre,
Or even felt interested in it
'Til this year. But I'm on my third sonnet
Of the morning before it's nine o'clock.
There's something about the direct address
That I have stolen, wholesale, from James Nash.
But I have also just realised that
My lack of ambition to be clever
Also presumes that you're hearing these words,
Rather than reading them. I imagine
I've an audience, am speaking aloud.
How long it has taken me to learn this!
My shrink sits across from me in her chair,
Listening and laughing when I tell her.

55: Forty-One

A whole year has passed, since we last made out,
Whilst my family sat down, near, to eat.
Tomorrow, we go wild swimming again.
I have placed on my dining-room table
A stone from the beach, a crystal, a shell:
He brought them all back from Australia.
His life goes on somehow in South London.
I wonder where he is and how he feels.
I must let go of my sadness before
My nephews arrive. My fantasy world
Already empty for fear I will dream
Of the colours and contours of his form.
I can't go back, can't go on without your
Red threads pulling me into the future.

56: Speech Act

From a pornotopian perspective,
It would probably come as a surprise:
He would only let himself come inside
My mouth once. I knew that it had happened
First in my throat. The sensation was odd –
Swallowing something I hadn't tasted
First. But then my activated palette
Responded to the love that we had made.
I could not get the salt of him out of
My mouth all day, or the catch from my throat.
Lately, I find that it is much the same:
My famished heart hungers for him again,
Hopes for a conversation, a text, word:
Melancholic, if it wasn't so rude.

57: The Goddess of Small Things

Three mint, peppermint; lemon and ginger,
Chamomile and lavender. Morning Time,
Sleepy Time. Three tulsi tea, whatever
That is. South African red bush; Love and
Harmonise. A tin of sweet osmanthus.
White tea, green tea, Earl Grey and Lady Grey.
Assam, Darjeeling, some Lapsang Souchong.
Treasured Habitat mugs from the nineties.
Fine china cups, patterned with Islamic
Geometric forms, white and peacock blue.
In a lesbian world, this may be the
Single most lesbian thing about me.
I try to end every day, I tell her,
Counting up the small things that kept me here.

58: Marsyas

Unlike last year, the sun did not stay out
On my birthday, and the cold waves that day
At Scarborough were six to eight feet high.
Nevertheless, Connor, Dylan and I
Were determined to spend time in the sea.
We each struggled to put on our wetsuits.
The three of us could not keep our balance,
Needed support from a nearby adult.
Wading into the water was hard work,
A strong tide pulling us across the bay.
Worth it to have that aerated, chill, salt
Foam thrown against us, to be hurled aground.
I got home, hung my wetsuit on the line,
The image of Marsyas's flayed skin.

59: Tales of the Avunculate

These days, Dylan is posing hard questions,
The kind to which there's no easy answer.
For example, coming back from the pool,
He asks me: "Where is your and daddy's dad?"
I honestly don't know what I will say.
"Neither of us are in touch with him: he
Was not a very nice man". (Not a beat).
"Was he kind to your mum?" "Especially
Not to her". "So they were not married for
Very long?" (Straight out of the mouths of babes!)
I laugh, because how on earth to explain
Why they stayed together over decades?
His own parents, thank god, so unlike this;
Still hope that he turns out different again.

60: Trans

In the same conversation, Dylan asks
"Why do you have that blond lady as your
Facebook picture? I asked mummy but she
Did not know". I try to be nonchalant,
Though I am a little discomforted:
"She's just a singer that I really like".
He asks "Does mummy know her?" "Don't think so".
Again, how to explain, that when I look
In the mirror, I expect to find there
Either Shawn Colvin or Emily Haines
Smiling at me, recognising my face
As their own. Also, I still don't know what
To do when Betsy says that she see there
A handsome man, sitting opposite her.

61: Earring (for Alison)

Observant, Dyl sees me in a new light.
"Why do you wear an ear-ring?" he inquires.
I think, reply: "It makes me look pretty".
I wonder how much sense this makes to him.
My brother then asks: "When did you get that?"
"Fifteen years ago, on the Cowley Road
In Oxford, in nineteen ninety-seven,
With Alison". I laugh. "It's not recent".
Can it be true my brother has never
Noticed this piercing in all the time we
Spent together over the last decade
And a half? And why does he now see it?
Eve calls this: "the simple material
Metamorphoses of everyday life".

62: Beard

"Have you ever thought of growing a beard?"
Betsy asks, liking the salt and pepper
Stubble growing from my face. I look down.
Once again, she hits the nail on the head.
A week spent thinking about cable-knit
Mariner's jumpers, also middle-aged
Lesbians whose cropped silver, grey and black
Hair I know that I have always admired.
How can my transference be so precise
Even given the clear visual cues?
Is it time I started to look my age?
I began to embrace my four decades
Of experience? Owned up to being
A professor? Mr. Jason Edwards?

63: Open

For the first time, on my way out of the
Tuesday session, I do not close the door.
For the last six months, each week, I get up,
Put on my coat, and pack up my baggage,
Then quietly shut her in. Suddenly,
This strikes me: a puzzling thing to do.
I recognise I've been trying to take
Up as little space as is possible,
To tune out the resonance in the air
Between us. "I'm going to leave the door
Open", I say, as an experiment,
At the very end of the next meeting.
On my way down the stairs, I feel somewhat
Exposed. I also cannot stop smiling.

64: Hiding in Plain Sight

For days now, I have been wanting to hear
Joni Mitchell's 'Moon at the Window' and/
Or 'Song for Sharon'. It is only when
I finally find a time to do so
That I understand why: "Betsy" appears
In both tunes: blue in one, seeking something
Good; suggesting finding a charity,
Work in ecology in the other.
(Joni wants to find another lover).
My Betsy wants me to buy a new coat
And shoes, which I dutifully do. It's
Stressful; but worth it when they are admired.
There is no more hiding in plain sight, but
I realise that I might quite like that.

65: Dining Room

We're drifting into a conversation
That we both had not anticipated.
She's puzzled: "Why not use your dining room?"
"Because it was my brother's space for years,
The place where I have failed to file my junk
And I don't keep the radiator on".
Like a startled mammal, her ears prick up.
Nosing out a sackcloth and ashes scene,
She's encouraging: "Start living in there".
So I turn on the heat, open the blind,
Evacuate the crap, pay attention
To what's on the walls: three gloomy seascapes
By Winslow Homer. Then I realise:
I've got resources that I haven't used.

66: Pan-Asian Lunch

I'm having, with Iz, a pan-Asian lunch,
The second, successive meal in two days.
It feels like throwing caution to the winds:
Might she not be bored if I'm not in pain?
It seems the universe has other views:
The waiter seems for me to have a shine;
The waitress is sparkling at Izzy.
It is only the couple behind us
That is having a polite argument:
"I told you that I love you", he insists.
The comforts of miso, fried rice and juice
I have known now for some twenty-five years.
I forget my gloves, nearly don't walk back,
But return, I've already lost too much.

67: Retrospect

An unexpected snowfall overnight
Leads to lots of posting upon Twitter,
So much astonishment, so much delight;
Lovely photo of Meg at the Minster,
Snowflakes on her lashes, eyebrows, and hair.
A lot of good timing, I realise:
Last weekend, I brought a new winter coat.
I bought in the geraniums last night.
Today, I went out walking after lunch,
Squinting in the blinding gold of dusk light;
Paused to by some flowers at the market.
When I got home, arranged them in a vase.
All of that time I wasted on Grindr,
I could have been buying myself a rose.

68: Osmanthus (for Izzy)

Last year, Izzy got me a birthday gift:
An exquisite glass teapot made for one.
With it came some sweet Osmanthus flowers.
I have not once used it in all that time.
One day, I thought of showing my nephews
How it worked: the way the flower first sinks
Into the water, right to the bottom,
And then slowly unfolds at its own pace.
Sepals and petals open themselves up.
Next, the orange clitoral stamen pops
Out, releasing an inverse shower of
Gold blossoms that rise to the water's brim.
Held expansively within the glass's
Containing frame: the ritual of our bloom.

69: What You Keep and What You Throw Away

This morning, I get up at six o'clock,
Have breakfast, as usual, sat on a chair:
A bowl of cereal, two cups of tea,
The cat mewing for milk at my cold feet.
Then I spend five hours cleaning up the house,
Two black bin bags full of rubbish, two more
For the R.S.P.C.A.; say goodbye
To that old green duffle coat, buttons lost;
Give to Oxfam a pile of paperbacks;
Polish the table, kneel upon the floor;
Place the silk throws in the washing machine;
Toss away every pair of socks with holes.
I notice that the clocks go back today,
For months, this stuff's been getting in my way.

70: Being Held and Being Dropped

Helen asks me "What are the differences
Between clear boundaries and withholding?"
"The former are enabling and kind,
In the latter case, someone is grasping
All the power". Helen wonders aloud:
"But can you control how others respond?"
I think probably not, but I ponder
Whether there is a difference in tone
That sounds the original intention
In the midst of all of that projection?
The distinctions, they are so fine between
Being held, being dropped, being picked up;
Withholding, withdrawing; holding, clinging;
Progression, regression, and aggression.

71: Shit Happens

Does he remember fucking that morning,
How shamed I felt when he slowly withdrew,
And the semen-filled end of the condom
Also had traces of shit upon it?
He was kind to me, made of it a joke:
"An occupational hazard", he said.
"What some people in the trade call code brown".
I laughed, but I was truly mortified.
Each day, my walk to work is a slalom
Through dog shit, and I pan-handle cat shit
From the tray, taking it to the dustbin.
The skylights? a bird-shit Pollock canvas.
I wish I could forgive myself and him,
I hope I'm able to say: "shit happens".

72: Queer/Animal

I woke this morning from the strangest dream:
I was standing in the hallway, shirt-less,
And a cat that was not quite or just mine,
Stretched itself up, roughly licked my nipple.
At the time it all felt so natural.
Although I did not lactate, surely an
Image of breast-feeding, myself as a
Mother, but also a little sexual.
One of my favourite erotic tropes,
Someone touching the very tip of me,
Their tongue against all of those nerve endings:
The synchronous density of neural
Firing. The cat was purring on my hip,
Blinking slowly at me, when I woke up.

73: In Which They Finally Make Contact

I can't have him and I can't stop crying.
Whatever was there in the summer's gone.
Apart as long as we were together.
With his boyfriend as long as we were friends.
Awkward, he pulled back, fearing how painful
It might have been for me; should have repaired
The breach more fully; be great to see me.
I genuinely don't know what to say.
Composed, I write back later in the day,
Tell him I'm sincerely happy for him,
What an annus mirabilis it's been,
Hopes his boyfriend knows how lucky he is.
And then it's over. The ball's in my court.
I'm all alone, again, to work this out.

74: Punctum

I see you out of my office window,
One of your ex-lovers is cycling past.
You exchange greetings, suddenly look shy,
So you turn your attention to your texts.
In observing this scene, I know at last
That I wouldn't swap all the time we've spent,
For the one night stands you had in the past;
That we have more sustained intimacy.
Don't get me wrong, though, I'd like to kiss you,
And though I see more clearly now your flaws,
Your oversized head and lumpy body,
If I'm watching porn, all I have to do
Is think of your mole-constellated skin,
Tongue, saliva, semen, and I just come.

75: Juarrez

Can just the thought of her going away
For a week at the end of October
Work to unravel me so completely
And return me to El Paso airport
Alone, homeless, at the end of August?
Or is it because I have to see him
At a seminar this coming Tuesday
And I fear that his boyfriend may be there?
It has been four months since we last texted
On a daily basis. I never thought
He'd disappear so completely from here.
I start to cry, whatever the reason;
Reach for Juarrez, that Tori Amos song,
"Dropped off the edge again; no angels came".

76: Conversation

Tuesday evening, at my invitation,
You're stood next to me, giving a paper.
You're articulate on conversation,
Which you describe in the following terms:
As something non-morally judgmental,
And also non-teleological.
Ideally, it's less like an argument,
And, if good, more like a mutual gamble
In which no one is seeking to persuade,
And both parties just listening, quite hard.
Alone together, after the lecture,
I'm handing you glasses, you're washing them.
When I cut myself, beyond intimate,
You know just where to find the first aid kit.

77: Appetite

It's only when we sit down to dinner,
That I remember how you make me lose
My appetite. The waiter comes over,
And asks if we'd like to have a starter.
I decline, and you order bruschetta.
I pick something simple for my main course.
You take more time, consult the specials board,
Choose food that'll take effort to prepare.
You also select a bottle of white,
Where I might have allowed myself a glass.
When the food arrives you offer me half;
A bit shaky, I'm able to accept.
Not sure I could ever have said before
"I love the way he thought of me, such care".

78: Held in Mind

We both have trouble keeping the other
In our minds when we are not together.
For you, it's as if no time is passing,
I'm always in the background, not pressing.
For me, out of sight is out of your mind,
And certainly, I fear, I might lose mine.
But when we meet up again on Tuesday,
I find your idiom full of my words,
And you remember everything I've said
Even if you'd had quite a lot to drink.
You let me know how, in your poetry,
You resist the first person singular,
Preferring a hard-won variety.
You're not forgetting, but repressing me.

79: The Middle Term

Something important about perspective
In what you say about the middle term.
I have never thought about this before
But it strikes me: a good lesson to learn.
The way that some good friendships then crumble,
Some are clearly destined to last a life,
Whilst others only come into their own
After a while, and that is the moment
In which you can suddenly feel secure,
You can rely upon the loyalty
Of people who've seen you really fuck up,
Of friends you may even have fucked over.
I think you're telling me that you're sorry,
That you might be in it for the long haul.

80: Easy

My masseur coaxes me: "Use your left hand
To pour the kettle or pick up a cup".
Izzy suggests that I let myself graze,
And, to make it easy, order food in.
This autumn of minute changes unfolds
With more deceptively simple advice.
I'm in the world again for the first time
Learning about what my body can do,
Feeling how I have a body, perhaps.
 "Why go back to work", Victoria asks,
"After the massage?" So I come straight home,
Make a cup of tea with the wrong hand, and
Play Tift Merritt, a little Aimee Mann;
Then, lo and behold, things look much less bad.

81: Gamelan

One hundred glass bells, each a condom tip,
Float and sway below St Mary's rooftop.
A full gamelan orchestra evokes
The percussive texture of rafter rain:
Intermittent, complex patterns emerge
In different instrumental sections.
Each piece ends with a gong's deep resonance.
A stillness in my chest. Sound dies away.
The musicians circulate, seat themselves
In another performer's space, pick up
What the last player has just lowered down,
Their palms' intimate heat democratic.
In media res, encouraged to leave:
Experience rests in our memories.

82: Foot Fetish

It might have taken me six or so months,
But on my way to my desk this morning,
I noticed that my feet were really cold,
I felt I should take better care of them.
Then rooting through the crowded junk cupboard,
I found slippers bought for me one Christmas,
A gift I'd found difficult to accept,
Like my shrink's belief I need not suffer.
These days, I am not falling down the stairs
So much, I try to descend carefully.
All of this kindness was waiting for me;
Just had to find a way to let it in.
My feet are not less important than his,
I can love us both equally, it seems.

83: Little Perennials

These small changes come with some growing pains:
I am having to learn to walk again
Because of the slight heel on my new boots
Which have somehow changed the length of my stride.
So I walk more confidently forward,
But I've got plasters all over my feet.
The wool coat's cut has changed my silhouette.
Why have I not, 'til now, bought clothes that fit?
The effect of this is remarkable,
Like a thrusting little perennial
Through the cold soil, surprising every spring.
It may not make a difference to him,
But Izzy's not the only one who's said
"You have never been more in your own skin".

84: Epiphany

I could have cried, on the way home Friday,
When Izzy conceded she'd do the gig,
"You're not fully out of this yet", I said.
I texted her, "I'm here if you need me".
But things were not as bad as they first seemed,
She'd hold her nerve, maintain her boundary,
Tell her bipolar ex girlfriend, who made
Her homeless again, the end of last week,
That she'd stay at her own place this weekend.
We went to the cat's rescue sanctuary,
And there met another abandoned stray.
After just a little hesitancy,
What unfolded was a joyful three-way:
A change not one of us could have foreseen.

85: Baby Talk

Izzy's sweet talking a cat with no name,
Who's hiding under her bed, the first day.
Neither of us had thought how traumatic
For this cat to be in a carrier,
An abandoned creature whose history
Includes being thrown and sealed in a box
And left for dead outside of M&S.
The cat is slowly but surely coaxed out
By the low tones of her mistress's voice.
Lying next to her, on the bedroom floor,
I find I'm thinking about baby talk.
How much my own cat likes sweet ladies' tones,
How much it pleases me and makes me cringe.
As a baby boy, did I hear such things?

86: Muse (for Victoria)

A conversation with VC has me
Musing on the different ways we receive
One another, starts me thinking about
Connections between sexuality
And creativity. For example,
Does your boyfriend find himself compelled to
Write sonnets each time that he talks to you?
Am I creatively oriented
To you as much as erotically?
No wonder I've found this so difficult
To give up on. Last week, over dinner,
You and I came quite close to knowing this,
When I told you that being a poet
Was my deepest, longest-surviving wish.

87: Blindsided

Claire praises my hair spontaneously,
She thinks that it makes me look much softer.
"You look beautifully ordinary"
My shrink says, after some ten days away.
"Your hair has grown a little bit longer,
Is less of a statement". I touch my face.
"Yes, and I haven't shaved for a few days".
My cropped head spoke of concentration camps,
Chemo, and recovering from cancer.
I honestly hadn't thought about this,
How I'd appear in the session today.
I get up to go, think I'll fall over.
I have to crouch down on the landing floor,
On the pavement when I get out her door.

88: And Relax...

I can see that I've been moving toward
This double massage session for a while;
From when she picked up on what I had said
About how I could monitor the time
That was passing through the guitar music.
Alarm bells also went off in her head
When I said how interesting I found it.
"Maybe you should come for two hours, instead
Of one hour twice next week, so you switch off?"
The experience: a sustained journey,
In some ways, beyond tolerance, such that
Each time that I felt this is good enough,
She did not stop; I became a witness
To a world of tenderness and kindness.

89: Lost in the Supermarket

Dyl is struggling to pronounce the name
Of the supermarket: calls it "wait-ross".
His vowels resonate; unexpected
Regional variant from lord knows who?
My shrink's shopping there on Sunday morning
With her spouse, whilst I have brunch with Izzy.
In succession, my face apparently
Blushes red, drains of blood, then turns quite blue.
In the session, a reparative game:
Shopping together, working out what age
I'd like to be: "A baby?" "So abject".
"A couple?" "Too old. Holding hands, age five".
"What would you like for your tea?" she asks me.

90: Vulpine/Hometime

4.40: about ten minutes to go
Before we have to say goodbye at the
End of the session. Out of the window
I see that it's gotten dark, car headlights
Visible across the park. My shrink asks:
"J, what does this time of day mean to you?"
"It feels good, like those moments I am home,
When I close the blinds, the heating comes on,
I burn incense, light tea-lights, turn on lamps,
Play choral music, maybe take a bath".
It also means a sore separation;
As I'm sent away, the night closes in.
Walking to my house, like a wary fox,
Making eye contact, scavenging for scraps.

91: A Dazzle of Zebras

When I bought that postcard of a zebra,
It was a snowy day in New Haven,
And I was on my way to the airport,
Relieved, at last, to be travelling home.
It comes to your address, ten months later,
With twenty pounds, for my half of dinner.
Five days pass; and then you send me a text.
"Hey J., thanks for the cheque. Very thoughtful
Of you. But how about I tear it up,
And you pay for the next meal? [Winking face]."
"Sounds like a good plan to me, just didn't
Want to leave you short in year four. Plus that
Zebra had your name on it, I reckon".
You reply; I'm hard as a pan-handle.

92: Hello Mr. Zebra

Straight after this short exchange, on my wall
You post a video of a French band,
Singing about zebras, too cool for school.
To which I immediately respond,
Tori singing Hello Mr. Zebra,
Fiona getting the thing that she wants.
The sexual undercurrent's palpable,
The riveting rivulets of her stripes.
And then it's as usual, nothing happens,
My heart's expectations are raised, it hurts.
I hadn't paid sufficient attention
When you told me how you loved serial
Music, the way that it interrupted
Expectations, turned habits on their head.

93: In Which the Poet Writes from the Depressive Position

Having seen you, the over-riding way
I feel is newly open to the world.
Vulnerable, for sure, and, if I'm honest,
More hopeful again, not trapped in the pain
Which had the virtue of composing me
At least, of braiding tight my warp and weft;
Whereas there's something fraying about this.
If the recto of hope's anxiety,
The verso of vulnerability
Cannot be said to be security.
Lying in bed, I tried something risky:
I held you in mind and masturbated.
Couldn't access the hurt from the near past,
But a relief to feel so loved at last.

94: Long Life

The final time we'll meet's been on my mind
This week: a palpable sense of relief
In your voice; now that your apprenticeship
Is really done, you are free to move on.
"I've loved every single moment we spent
Together over the last eighteen months.
I just wish that there had been more of them,
And that less time had passed between each one.
The only thing that is getting me through
Is the hope that, with a carrying wind,
It's a long life, and that I'll continue
To be able to keep on seeing you.
Can I hug you, rest my head on your chest?"
So much that might have been, so much now lost.

95: Things That Matter

Connected somehow, three related scenes:
You are stood at an adjacent lectern,
I'm unable to look up at your face,
Though I glow in your luminous presence,
Find I am fully steeped in your deep voice.
Izzy is sat a musician away,
Singing the song she has composed for me.
I sit very still in the candlelight,
My face blood-burnished, my hands prayer like.
"I feel intensely self-conscious this week.
It is excruciating". My shrink asks:
"What would a six year old say about this?"
Tough to find the words: "It's hard in some ways
Loving him, not easy how much she cares".

96: Ark

Somewhere deep within, tectonic plates shift;
Rocks crack, waves break; Pangaea starts to split;
Oceans where continents were in my heart;
Ecological clusters drift apart;
Key populations have remained intact;
Creatures with new neighbours eye each other,
Pause to ascertain the pecking order;
Some species disappear, others resurge;
In old niche spaces, new critters emerge;
At first, look like family relations,
But given more careful observations,
Behold: miraculous interruptions!
What happened whilst I was asleep last night?
Who's fashioned this ark that keeps me afloat?

97: Precedent (for Sarah Monks)

It takes a lot of energy, I find,
To make precedent: to even notice
What's going on is tough enough at first
And this is before you try to dislodge,
Then haul up, through the dead weight of water,
Your old, barnacle-encrusted anchor.
After that, you have to wait on the wind,
To ascertain how to angle canvas.
In the misted air of the mid-pack ice,
You need to have command of your whole boat,
To know how to read the stars, a compass,
To heave yourself across magnetisms,
With enough flexibility to dodge
The icebergs of your ingrained tropisms.

98: Wound

Eve says "Sometimes a scar is just a scar".
Here, another story has been revealed:
He takes his mobile phone from his pocket -
A spider web: the cracked glass of the screen.
I shudder at the sheer amount of blood,
Don't initially recognise his arm.
He says he broke a cup and stabbed himself,
In his frustration, with one of the shards.
"You look as if you are going to cry",
And it's true that my eyes are full of tears.
Less to reassure me than to shut down
The whole subject, a heartbreaking gambit:
"The scar is just a scar", he seems to say,
But it took five stitches at A and E.

99: A Poet is Being Beaten (for Paul)

Some days, my parents would thrash my bottom,
On others, dad would hit me in the head.
Remember, also, that living room scene,
Where our mother had to drag off our dad
But not before the bruising had occurred?
A miracle he didn't break a limb.
They had to keep you from primary school,
Shorts, uniform short-sleeved-shirts would reveal,
And there might be trouble, even back then.
Slapped, my right ear throbbed, temple hurt like hell.
Immediately, though, I found I thought:
Beat me all you like, you will never win,
I am not beaten when I am beaten,
I'll swallow your blows, start my life again.

100: Bodhisattva

There are times I need to own my power,
Others when it's fine to help you stack chairs,
To give you a hand after the lecture,
So no one would guess I'm a professor.
I like to be the one to serve the wine
At my own events, before stepping up
To the lectern, so I can introduce:
Witness the surprise on that young man's face,
Or the quiet, fine line between managing
Confidently, inconspicuously.
What happens when I love someone deeply?
I make myself invisible, become
Audience and host. You don't see me top
Your cup with the milk of human kindness.

101: The View from Two South Bank Deck Chairs

Here, he was always ahead of the game:
When it came to the ideology
Of the simultaneous orgasm,
He was relaxed about the sequential.
So many poems on the difference
Between my knowing and realising,
And still I find myself surprised at this,
At not having put together these things.
One of the lessons of being single,
Of no longer being in a couple:
If we don't, these days, share adjacency,
Spatially, temporally, affectively;
At random moments, many months apart,
We can still come together in our hearts.

102: Izzy Isgate and the Masturbating Boy

Generative, the muse of masturbation.
In public, a private conversation,
At lunch, we talk about "self-relation".
Mornings, I turn on my computer screen,
The rich ecology of online porn,
Thousands of obscene bodies to be seen.
Some days, it's just bodily sensation:
Exhaling, ready for the reception,
Clench kindly, to embrace the insertion.
Sometimes, I use my imagination
To generate a representation.
At nights, I dream: as an illustration,
We make love in the most vanilla scene,
Entwined in missionary position.

103: In Which the Poet Uses Skype for the Second Time

I have never much liked using the phone,
Although this has gotten worse over time.
Fearful of unwelcome interruption,
With no sense that I could just be ignored.
Sara and my friendship has nearly stalled
A number of times, because it's so bad.
But in the interests of live relation,
Of spontaneous communication,
I install Skype, say I'll give it a go.
Sara says she looks forward to seeing
My face on the screen. This I am hearing
With surprise. Why have I never felt so?
It's not like looking in the mirror, then;
She looks back with love, I don't seem alone.

104: Leaf Print

I don't know how it happened, but it did.
Not a single mark on the stair carpet
But a perfect leaf print upon her floor
Which sits like the throb of shame in my face.
I apologise, say it wasn't meant.
My shrink hears me, holds out for something else.
The law of unintended consequence,
Literally millions of words in Proust,
Still I find myself totally bemused.
Could there be a better metaphor for
My spoiling, aggressive attack on her?
For my unconscious being-in-the-world?
She can still hear the anger in my voice,
But holds me firmly until it has passed.

105: The Music of the Spheres

We meet, the first floor of the Berwick Saul.
I ask if you're feeling any better?
Delighted to be back in your orbit,
Within your strong, gravitational pull.
At the day's end, a familiar risk:
When I get back home, I send you a text,
Thank you for inviting me to dinner,
Suggest you should recuperate and rest.
"I will heal and be nice and fulfill all
My obligations. I can have it all".
(Yes, in my sunny Copernican view).
After so much time, the things I've been through,
My being straightforwardly kind to you
Still feels like the most loving thing to do.

106: Don't Take My Love For Granted

"Do not take my love for you for granted"
Is what (I'm afraid) I'm trying to say.
"I know fan is my default idiom,
But please hear this: you're truly valuable."
You laugh, counter: "remember at dinner,
You found almost everyone stupid, dull?"
You recognise that you're exceptional.
Earlier in the summer, you described
How fast I'd become indispensable
To your life. So I was, erm, promptly dropped.
Caring for you, a fraught line for us two:
Risking self-destruction, powerful use.
In myself, I need to find more trust, faith.
Let's try to take better care of us both.

107: Lukewarm

You're describing bending the universe
To your will. Four days later, I can hear
The queer resonance of that word "bending"
In tales where you're seducing your straight friend.
I suggest the patient, passive pleasures
Of waiting for fate to meet you half way.
Imagining sexual epiphany,
Finding the erotic ordinary,
Embracing relationality there.
Fifteen years ago, when I was younger,
I waited for years for Luke to want me.
When push came to shove, he couldn't kiss me.
Your straight boy sex also disappointing.
For us, a different kind of relating.

108: Hot

It's 2 a.m., we are in the cold street,
Breath pluming as we drift down Goodramgate.
I regret the v-neck cut of my coat,
Your bare chest revealed by your open shirt.
True, then, your bodily temperature
Maintains you two or three degrees higher
Than us mere mortals; you're even hotter,
If that is possible, than you appear.
That you find it hard to sleep, no wonder,
You must sweat under the lowest togged quilt.
We hug briefly at the end of our date;
I think you might have asked if I hadn't.
Embracing me, you seem lighter, slighter.
I can't rest in bed, my love burns brighter.

109: In Which the Poet Embraces his Masculinity

Izzy's characterised me as the most
Lesbian person she has ever met.
Increasingly, the phrase doesn't quite fit.
I want her to describe me as a man.
One reason I'm so attracted to him:
How much his conversation's full of men.
Friday night's I like to go drink with him,
Wake up hung over the following morn.
He and his straight boy wake up in a spoon,
Whereas he and I each awake alone.
I feel like a loyal dog with a bone,
Heart's so full of love, I fear it'll burst.
Don't know how to get release: should I come
Or let myself cry as much as I can?

110: In Which the Poet Recognises his Sibling Rivalry

I find myself competing, tallying
The things that hurt me by the afternoon:
The picture of your ex boyfriend out cold;
Excerpts from a conversation you shared;
As you both lay shirtless in the morning,
You delaying his day starting, playing
With his right nipple, a familiar,
Poignant scene: My Own Private Idaho;
That this had been going on for a year;
That my masseur might yet get to hold you,
Help release the tension in your shoulder,
Rub oil into your mole-barnacled skin;
The thought again of him "slipping you in".
This is a game that I can never win.

111: In Which the Poet Seeks Acceptance

Let me just say, I'm glad to have this day.
I used to dread alone time at weekends,
And I admit I feel fragile again
Now that Izzy may have found someone new,
Whilst you're going back to Australia
To see your folks a few short weeks from now.
The solstice looms bleak on my horizon.
How to survive another long winter?
I'll need to put some strategies in place:
Keep going to massage and therapy,
Learn to trust that I'm in all of your minds,
Show up when I'm invited out by friends,
Feel sad and happy each time that I do,
Accept what it means to keep loving you.

112: The Dark Lady

You're with a girl in your new photograph,
It's taken me a while to work out why.
Signature white t-shirt, your glasses off,
I wonder how much of him you can see.
I'd like to post, "Gosh, you look so handsome",
To strip you down, right there, to your slim waist.
Your ex-boyfriend comments here: "UNF"
(Meaning "Universal Noise of Fucking").
Over drinks on Friday, you're reporting,
In a club, seeing the longing of three
Women, then making out with each of them.
"I can do this too", you say to your friend.
My heart hurts: you and these women kissing,
All of your precious desire gone to waste.

113: Patchwork (for Victoria)

"Patchwork thematises the processes
Of rupture and repair, valorising
Complex and composite structures over
Other ideals: the brittle fantasy
Of the unbroken, or the ideal of
Monolithic integrity". (This speaks
To an idea that 'I' made long ago).
I barely pause for breath before writing:
"Eve would have agreed, and loved this sentence,
And so do I". In fact, I can't think of
A better way to describe her patchworks
Combining ragged scraps of kimono
Silk in various configurations.
I braid here our deft, three-way relations.

114: Bathroom Song

I trample mud on her carpet again.
My shrink seems non-plussed but interested.
I feel told off, fear I'm going to cry.
She notices, pauses, and steadies me.
Next time, I'll take off my shoes, we agree.
Just then, the fear really starts to kick in.
My comings and goings are already
So powerfully over-determined.
The amount of shame that's now in the room
Makes her ask about my toilet training.
An image of eating shit comes to mind.
I feel, in this scene, a lot of shouting.
No beaming smile for me on the potty;
Irritation from mummy and daddy.

115: Barefoot

At her door, I'm especially anxious.
After the two recent shitty sessions,
This, the first time I will take off my shoes.
Nothing's changed for her, she goes up the stairs,
Leaves me fumbling at my laces down here.
Arriving, in my socked feet, in the room,
I feel vulnerable and turned on at this
Asymmetric striptease revelation.
Now I can tuck my feet under my knees,
I'm able to relax on the settee
In quite a new way. I find I want to
Pirouette in the available space.
Still surprising, that such little changes
Can put me in this balletic new place.

116: Anniversary Card

To hold on too closely or for too long.
To be always affectively off key.
To be tone deaf and to sing out of tune,
Confidently, without realising.
To give your baffled parents poetry
And to feel, on their anniversary,
Shame bleeding out too fast for your blotter,
As you explain to your mum what it means.
The mortifying scene then repeated
When your father gets home from work at five;
Phrases pulsing in each capillary,
Indelible on your face, on the card.
How did my love for poetry survive?
And, given all this, how the fuck did I?

117: Come in from the Cold

"Jason, I'm afraid I'm going to need
Some taking care of this weekend. Are you
Free at all?" "Of course I am. How urgent
Is it?" "Moderately, I'm feeling bruised
More than anything acute. I wanted
To get out of the house last night and slept
(As much as I could) on a good friend's floor.
I'm just feeling discombobulated".
I'm crying, relieved you can turn to me.
A chance to fix the summer, a replay:
This time my need will not get in our way.
Tonight, you'll come round, and I'll fix some food.
We'll be happy as Larry and Joni
Gracefully dancing their way through the wood.

118: Alluvial

You describe two moments of seeing men
At a distance, who you knew you could have
In the end, although no one believed you:
Your current heterosexual best friend;
An ambiguous, not-fully-out boy.
I think of that day by the Berwick Saul,
Hope that I might be a third example.
No need for you to bind me to your will;
When it comes to you, I'm alluvial.
Move toward me at your glacial pace,
My geology is happily shaped.
I lie down, find I want to feel your weight;
Long for you to excavate a crevice,
To forge my landscape, fashion my surface.

119: Baritone Tenor

The thing about this picture I admire
Is not how carefully posed you appear,
Nor the focal play between the foreground
And the boy on the couch in the background,
But the hint of a neck of a guitar.
A week later, I ask, over dinner,
If, next time you come, you'll bring it along;
I will swap you a sonnet for a song.
(Round this, Izzy felt under-confident).
Of course, you tell me, you're a good singer.
Beneath the self-regard, though, something else:
You say that, when playing your instrument,
A vibrato manifests in your voice,
Just appears there, doesn't give you a choice.

120: Lap Dog

You like talking about your erections,
How, in the mornings, you get wood, lying
In bed, pressed against your straight friends, spooning.
You also reveal you get a hard on
In galleries, looking at each picture.
This isn't a hard one for me to hear
About: I wonder, is it like children
Being happily held; the place swimming
In warm and diffuse eroticism?
You say you're attracted to everyone.
What's my place in your imagination?
Just another, sad tantalised voyeur?
After all, I'm an art historian.
This poem sucks the marrow from that bone.

121: In which my Benefactor Pauses for Thought

Whilst we are talking, I begin to see
The way in which not just your expression,
But your whole face changes; it's as if I
Speak to a number of different boys.
All the while, literally for many hours,
You look apart, legs crossed towards the door.
Around the end of the conversation,
You and I make recursive eye contact.
At the close of the evening, comes a pause.
You think hard about where you'd like to rest.
Before you decide that you will go home,
We make up the bed, imaginatively;
In the morning, I bring you hot green tea.
I lay my head on your chest, you hold me.

122: Blind Spot

Sent you a picture after our first date
Of the cat trying to sleep on my hip,
Explained she was good at keeping me warm;
The first move to which you didn't respond.
I found it hard to believe that you weren't
Attracted to me until you came round;
Didn't notice the cat around your feet,
Sidling up against your brown ankle boots.
Last week, you wrote about her in a text,
Then you made friends after dinner last night,
You talked about your family's two pets,
How usual for them to run up and greet
You. I must not allow myself to get
My hopes up yet: you still don't want a cat.

123: The Other Side of the World

" We are only playing" is what you said.
You want me to relax. I wish I could.
It's just that, once again, you disappeared.
I'm also conscious of my aggression
And my capacity for feeling hurt.
I still can't tolerate games of fort-da,
Fear my opponent will be gone for good.
The uncertainty of a flirtation
Brings up the ghosts of my abandonment.
Can I hope to learn relating from scratch?
Recover myself from forms of attack?
Would you hug me close 'til this fear burns out?
"Can you forgive my carefulness?" I ask.
After Australia, will you come back?

124: The Smell of a Hangover

Your friend isn't as hard as I expect,
The other doesn't seem so confident.
In fact, I suspect that the aggression
Of the straight boy Fight Club scene is your own.
You're clearly the centre of gravity,
And you must seem very grown up to them.
I see your friend crying, held in your arms;
The other praise the design of your room.
In spite of all the obvious vanity,
I find that it's the insecurity,
Naive earnestness that most touches me.
The shame you feel in your friend's description:
How, on the morning after our last date,
Hung over is the way your body smelt.

125: White Glasses

Two of my favourite people in the world
Sit across from me in this photograph.
They smile broadly, their shoulders adjacent.
Both seem to say, in their different ways,
Through smiles, eye contact, "I love you Jason".
As if to knock foreheads, Ben leans forward.
To see me better, Izzy leans right back.
They've swapped spectacles for my amusement,
This is the final time this'll happen.
Their perspectives will not converge again.
The melancholy piercing bouquet of
The two of them, looking at me with love.
This image provides me with such comfort,
A dyke and a fag as my queer parents.

126: Touching Feeling

Izzy's encouraging you, from over
By the young men that you really desire,
To join your friends, who've come to say goodbye.
Even then, I am sat too far away.
You couldn't be much more distant from me,
And I feel the panic rising inside;
Watch as Izzy admires your upper arm.
Is everyone pervious to your charm?
Not sure I could feel more sad or envy,
Your bicep flexes in her impressed palm.
I don't allow myself to touch your skin.
Sometimes your knee brushes up against mine.
Twice, I comfort you, palm against your spine,
And feel myself less achingly alone.

127: The One in which He Leaves for Australia

A public place with everybody
Watching us. There's just two things I can say:
"Keep in touch. Come back". (Your friend stands nearby).
You are trying to be reassuring.
You tell me that you will send me postcards.
I hope you'll replace your Sunday Skype slot
To your mum and dad with a call to me.
It's obvious to all that I am bleeding.
I sit, looking down, a half empty glass
Of something dark and sweet cupped in my hands.
Claire tells me Eoin doesn't compromise.
"Find somebody your own age", Kirstin hints.
I daren't look at Izzy sat opposite,
Fear there are tears welling in both our eyes.

128: Shakespeare

My Cambridge degree's not worth the paper
That it's printed on, since I did not know,
'Til I was over forty, that Shakespeare
Didn't write the plays he's credited for.
I avoided reading, purposefully,
The Sonnets whilst I was writing my own.
The definite article was reason
Enough: The Sonnets, not just some poems.
But they and these have something in common:
A charismatic youth, an older man;
May to December creativity;
A monument to love's futility.
When people say: "Aren't they about that boy?"
Shakespeare's sonnets will be my alibi.

129: The Poet Tells his Therapist about a Recent Dinner

Another difficult session with her,
In which, although my adult feels cared for,
My inner infant, he feels disciplined,
Learns he's envious, spoiling, even mean.
The hardest thing to hear: I'm demeaning.
Honestly, none of this is surprising.
I fully own it, although I hate it.
But I still want her to be on my side.
Reassuring, she doesn't move away.
She stays sitting there, looks me in the eye.
We are approaching a midwinter pause,
So everything feels raw, precarious.
I need her to tuck me into my bed,
To wrap me up like a Christmas present.

130: Stair Carpet

After the session, on my way down stairs,
I'm on the carpet for the hundredth time.
But it strikes me as something I've not seen,
Till suddenly I remember again
Exactly the same scene two days before.
Why have I repressed this detail so long?
I'm much less likely to slip and fall down,
It's safer to leave than I seem to know.
She's thought about her patients I would say!
I appreciate the traction given
By the pile of the hard wearing runner,
And the fact that I can quietly leave.
When loving kindness mostly fills her cup,
Why would I think she'd want to trip me up?

131: The Good Enough Breasts

My shrink wanted me to ask my mother
If I'd been breastfed as a little kid.
"No", my mum replied. "You were bottle fed".
(No surprises there). "And the other two?"
"Yes, they were". "Why was that?" (I had to ask).
"I tried to breastfeed your older brother,
But my nipples were too small". (That makes sense).
"When he was born, I tried again with Mike".
"What small nipples you have", my father said.
It made me wince, he cut me to the quick.
Must have hurt her too; it was designed to.
(My father was a nasty piece of work).
I loved Ben's nipples; it was voracious
How much I wanted to touch them, to suck.

132: Foreskin

It was only when Max referred to my
Idiosyncratic foreskin that I
Realised that there was something different
About my body: a tightness that meant
It could not be easily retracted.
He was not judgmental; he was gentle.
We were lying together in his bed.
In fact, I was in his arms, in his scent.
We were both sticky with each other's cum.
Still, it made me feel shamed as I walked home.
I took a long bath the following night;
A deep breath, gingerly eased the skin down.
This cut boy's care for me made me feel sad:
Why had I not been shown how by my dad?

133: Dildo Landfill, or, The Lesbian Phallus

An online lesbian forum pondered
The ethics of what to do with sex toys
When a relationship comes to an end.
Whether it was ok to carry them
With you into the subsequent bedroom
Or whether it was better to dispose?
A prosthetic or part of your body,
The funny way that the question was posed.
Someone, of course, raised the key green issues.
It made me laugh out loud to think of these:
Dildo landfill; a great name for a band?
An appropriate way to fill a space?
The ideal place for all those phalluses?
How do I love Izzy? Just count the ways.

134: Time Lapse (for Alison)

You do not want to talk about how much
Time has lapsed since we last saw each other.
I would say that we have not scratched this itch
For seven or more years, since before Ben.
You're right. We're instantly in present tense.
As we walk along the road from King's Cross,
It's as if not a single moment's passed.
Perceptive, you tell me how much I've changed,
That I seem more comfortable in my skin,
To have settled down inside of myself,
To have grown infinitely less anxious.
I'm delighted that this is so obvious.
For more than three decades, my oldest friend,
You've loved me: at forty one, eleven.

135: Argos

Setting off on another odyssey,
I check you have enough food and water.
I have arranged, each day, a visitor
In case the solitude leaves you lonely.
You get to stay at home, I catch a train,
Away overnight for work once again.
I wonder how the time feels in your mind,
Whether you can stay afloat or sink down?
I get out the taxi, run down the road,
Open the door, throw off my winter coat.
You're crying all the while behind the door.
I come in, lay next to you on the floor.
"Only death would stop me from coming home".
You're alongside me in every poem.

136: Killjoy (for Sara Ahmed)

How to tell my shrink that I've been dreaming
About how much I hate her these last days?
That I want to smash us to smithereens?
That I feel abandoned, sent back to school?
That I just want to lie down in the road?
How do I tell Iz that I've been hurting
Around the scene of her and Ben flirting?
(The same evening, grateful, as we have seen).
How on earth will I find the correct words?
I can only imagine these as cruel,
That they'll leave me feeling vulnerable.
But if I do not say these things aloud,
They'll come out in vicious, less conscious ways.
I have to keep my unconscious at bay.

137: Fish Story

The two of you started with the chorus,
Then kept on adding sweet descants from there.
No bridge, or sludgy verses to wade through.
No blue notes to wait through. Just harmonies,
Hooks upon hooks, with no fish getting killed.
Deliciousness of bait, being thrown back,
Ecstatically, and with no trace of lack.
The purpose of salmon swimming upstream;
The leap of flying fish above water;
The flash and slap of silver scales and fins;
The gasp of gills, swish of their golden tails;
Not so much armoured as flexing their mail.
Who wouldn't want to swim amidst their shoal?
Who wouldn't desire to be in their school?

138: The Good Surprise

On a lute, Paul plays an ostinato,
(Loaned from the Italian for stubborn),
A rising, repeating arpeggio.
I have always loved this early modern
Idiom, the way one's emotion is,
Through intervals, both evoked and contained.
Izzy tacitly asks: Can I cut in?
A nod of the head and she joins the dance,
Adding acoustic guitar, alto voice
Across two verses. The second, spanking,
Percussive; her instrument responding
With the same smile of recognition as
Beams from my face, and the audience's:
A quartet performing the good surprise.

139: Elementary

Not sure who I identify with most:
Facilitative, not quite romantic,
But certainly intimately involved
Watson. Or the easily bored, crazy-
Intelligent boy-in-a-man's-body:
Charismatic, borderline autistic
Sherlock Holmes. The boarding-school back-story
Also evocative. I'm a sucker
For such privately educated men,
Whose breathless speech just keeps up with their thoughts,
And who offer tantalising trickles
Of relationality in the form
Of adjacency, and calculated
Revelation along with instruction.

140: All the Vicious Things

That Christmas after I came back from school
For the first time, everything fell flat;
I think I'm still recovering from that.
I stepped into my reassuring role,
But my parents didn't need comforting;
They had each other, they had lost nothing.
Where are my brothers in this memory?
In this bleak scene, there's just mum, dad and me.
I remember staring at fairy lights,
Hoping to feel alright, to see beauty,
Trying to find some kind of miracle.
There was no one else, I made do with God.
I hope that there was a cat on my bed,
Please forgive all the vicious things I said.

141: River

Sometime last winter, you gave a paper.
J. emailed later, said how good you were.
It was part admonishment and part pride –
Your fellow panellist's supervisor.
I meant to attend; as my alibi,
My official role as head of centre.
But the snow-fall was heavy, I was tired.
Late December, you're in Australia.
Here, it keeps raining, there are gale force winds.
I'd relish the walk through the frozen air,
With my ipod on, to come and see you.
That, or skate along a frozen river:
A scene from Wordsworth's Prelude, Joni's Blue.

142: Triptych

A triptych of Canadian landscapes
Hang, framed in black, on my living room wall,
Each flecked with carmine leaves. The first snow fall
Of winter. Next, a February blue sky,
The sudden expanse of afternoon light.
Then, a river's thrust and gush, free of ice.
Although moving through late autumn to spring,
The way is blocked in each of the pictures:
A row of birches interrupts the view,
Stops the route to the hills in the first two;
A precarious balance of foreground
In the third, that cold water rushes by.
Wind-blown snow, like feathers from the goose-grey
Heavens; leafless bones; ice-scoured river stones.

143: Tom Thomson, *A Northern Lake* (c.1916)

In this small painting, the sun is setting,
More than half of the image a pink sky.
A rocky promontory not much of a
Foreground; a dark forest in the mid-ground.
The waves on the glacial-blue lake, like ice.
The painter needs to pack up his 'canvas',
(Oil paint on a composite wood pulp board),
And hurry home. It looks like mid-winter.
Not long left to canoe through the water.
Now the light is going, the air gets cold.
You feel it first as a burn on your face,
Then your core temperature starts to drop;
Lungs so cold only a bath warms you up;
Only then does your mind regain its grip.

144: Tom Thomson, *Northern Lights* (1916 or 1917)

Hard to tell if the six patches of paint,
In no particular constellation,
Are falling snow or are stars in heaven.
A diagonal line of three appear,
On second glance, descending to the right;
Still don't clinch the case, but seem more like stars
In their turbulent vat of indigo.
Straight out of the Somme, blasted foreground trees.
Snow on the shore, floating on the water.
Not much between frozen trunks and driftwood.
A horizontal, high-lit orange line,
An oaring man standing on a slim boat?
The northern lights - icicle stalagmites.
A cold night past, or ahead, in a tent.

145: Tom Thomson, *Moose at Night* (Winter 1916)

I wonder if you slept so silently
That this pair of regal, ice-blue-assed moose
Brushed right past your tent, quite oblivious
To your presence there. Did they disturb you?
By then, you knew, quickly, to move gently
If you were to paint what had wandered past.
The sound of stepping, breathing, and sloshing.
In this case, a vision composed the view:
An antlered male admires the firmament;
A female trails behind in the river.
A pair of wise ones following the star;
A Canadian holy family
On their journey to the nativity.

146: *Algonquin*

Hard winter, 1916-17:
Across the Atlantic and the Channel,
A battle of exploding mud and wood.
In his winter coat, he'd each time set out
With nothing but a tent in his row boat;
Hand-painted demijohn, decorated
Pannikin; a light travelling suitcase,
With a leather strap and a belt buckle,
Trebling up as a palette, an easel,
The lightest of back packs. An oar, oil tubes;
Perhaps a fishing rod to catch trout with.
Firewood, he'd gather as he needed it.
Wondering each time, can I survive this?
As he set off again, will I come home?

147: A Case of You

So you've gone, though you said you'd stay in touch.
You're salt-bronzed in the southern hemisphere;
I'm wind-burned, constant as a northern star,
Aurora borealis in darkness,
A Tom Thompson winter arctic canvas;
A lonely painter, drowned in a river.
With your Irish-Australian background,
You drink me under the table each time;
Makes me wonder: how much you remember
Of the moments that we spent together?
The thought of your feet in these metric feet,
A wish to swallow you, salty and sweet.
I've nearly bled out once, and still I bleed,
Will you come back in January? God speed.

148: A Pair of Pots

Christmas Eve means it's also his birthday;
When I wake, he's the first thing on my mind.
Trying to decide whether it's better
To send him a text or post on Facebook.
Of course, I decide to do both. Why choose?
A short pause, then he sends me a text back.
"I am at my brother's, but miss my pots".
This refers back to the ceramic pair
That we bought near the British Museum
When we saw each other the last weekend;
One as a gift, one as its companion.
After all we've been through, all of this time,
Is it still so hard to say I love you?
Must he tell me in an indirect way?

149: Sonnet for Tanya

On Christmas morning, I woke to two texts
From half a world away, sending me love:
How much of the hot southern hemisphere
Came, in those messages, through the ether?
I was held in mind after all these months,
By a friend I've met half a dozen times,
Who, in the summer, just transformed my life
With that black box workshop where I lay down,
Rested my head on that boy's lower back,
Was fully embraced by that tall singer,
Entered the arms of Zoe and Lisa;
Izzy nearby, doing similar work.
The two of you briefly met each other,
She understood why I'd wish you'd been there.

150: A Postcard from New Mexico (for Stephanie)

As I began considering the end
Of this sequence, of this nine-month process,
I knew that I couldn't finish without
Sending a postcard from New Mexico.
I remember, in a bar, telling Ben
How important the experience was,
Of arriving somewhere quite different,
And finding I could start my life again;
A quiet way of letting him know how bad
Things seemed in August, how much I'd been hurt.
Stephanie met me at the airport gate,
When she saw me, couldn't have been more glad.
Finn slept soundly on the floor by my bed,
Woke me in the night, licking my armpit.

151: Solstice (In Memoriam)

These late December days, I go to ground.
I want to lay down for good in the cold
Bed, have the soil shoveled on top of me.
So many moments when the web, on which
I am poised, precariously, unhooks
From the tips of the branches, or is wrenched
Apart by a passing, well, anything.
For example, walking down Park Grove Street,
I see, after months of seeming silent,
That Sandra's house is advertised vacant.
This must mean that my allotment neighbour,
Who taught me so much, gave me all those plants,
Won't share a strawberry or raspberry,
Earthed from the ground, fresh from the cane again.

152: Fluffer

I've got to get you out of my system.
I've had enough and nowhere near enough.
You are split, cruel, fair-weather and half-baked.
When I saw the three separate faces
That passed across your visage when we talked,
Should've run for the hills, and not just wanked.
What is it about you that makes you think
That it is somehow fine to ignore me?
And what about me that makes it ok?
So fuck you and your untouchable face,
For posting sex talk on your Facebook page,
On the same day you didn't acknowledge
My Christmas greeting to you and your folks.
Once again, you've made me feel like a joke.

153: A Closet is like a Russian Doll

Consider, dear reader, my romantic
Minimalism; my chicken scratching
For scraps of your attention, compassion;
And the Darwinian competition
For discarded crusts of your affection.
Go back to my youth, you'll find a closet,
Section 28, a queer called Jason
Raped with a stick at my secondary school.
Still further back, you'll find more hungry birds:
My two brothers and I differently starved,
Hoping for my parents' interest, kindness.
What has come clear to me in your silence:
My need might be heard, briefly, but it won't
Be long held in your arms, let alone healed.

154: Endgame (for James)

At the time he wrote his sonnet sequence,
James said he recalled the precise moment,
After a lengthy apprenticeship, when
He suddenly grasped how the genre worked.
He felt that his mind had become hard wired
And poems began to pour out of him.
I find myself there in the present tense,
Not now waiting on a chance rhyme to come,
But working one up. It's precisely at
This point, when I have obtained fluency,
At the second I notice it's easy,
That I no longer feel like I'm at home,
Recognise that I am in an endgame,
That I'm compelled to seek another form.

III

Complexity, Death, and Nothing

Did they poison my food?
Is it because I'm a girl?
If I puked up some sonnets, would you call me a miracle?

Neko Case

A Change of Perspective

How come I never noticed this cafe?
A baby dyke and tattooed lesbian
Laughing over chai tea latte behind
The counter, Feist singing in the background
"You're breaking your heart, for a teenage boy".
Izzy and I are sat by the window,
A great view of the vegetarian
Cafe, the opposite side of the street,
Where we've eaten for a year, once a week;
Close by, The Habit, where Ben and I drank.
Outside, everybody looks like they're fit,
A metropolitan population.
We could be in London or in Brooklyn,
Suddenly, York appears quite different.

Advent Sonnet

The cold, pink light of a December dawn,
The stars begin to fade into the light.
Take this astronomical metaphor
To depict an astrological change:
The slow, sure lifting of a long-held curse,
The gradual shifting of the universe;
A new sense of personal gravity;
A renewed sense of possibility.
Tuesday is a therapy day, of course,
And I'm warm in spite of the iceberg foam
That floats upon this morning's bath water;
The radiator's also burning hot.
To be content these days, not even strange;
Thirteen days and the world will be reborn.

Aegis

I got to thinking about all the things
That queer men like to do with their semen:
The way in which his ejaculation
Basically stands in for urination,
A desire for subordination
Or for his partner's humiliation.
For me, it's all about lubrication
Or at least it was in our relation:
How I'd want him to come first on my groin,
Before using it on my tight foreskin;
Then, immediately after I'd come,
What intimate, sterile inter-minglings;
I would rub you into my abdomen,
An aegis from which we could both begin.

Aerial (Election Day, May 8 2015)

Claire's taught me to think in structural terms,
I realize how serious this is:
The Conservatives for the next five years,
Means further state-mandated eugenics.
Keep funding royal births in hospital,
Keep bailing out indifferent business,
And offer tax breaks to the very rich.
Let the frail and the ill go to the wall.
Let's raise a bitter glass, start the count down,
One-thousand-eight-hundred-and-twenty-four
Days until the general election.
In the meantime, appreciate the small
Changes in the pattern around us all.
Listen: a blackbird, on the aerial.

A File of Old Photos

Before things went so wrong, he was lovely:
He painted an oil portrait of me;
He framed a photo of us from New York,
Blurry from the close range, the light of dawn.
I was so afraid of sharing our bed,
I feared that the cat would feel rejected
And would not be able to understand.
And then I filled up our short life with work,
Took for granted our deep intimacy,
Dissolved a little more of us each day.
How little I forgave him that last year,
Drove him the 300 miles to London.
How much I loved him, from finger to ear,
How much I treasure our present-tense blur.

A Man Called James

"It looks like you're leaning in for a kiss,
In your profile picture", I say to him;
A wiry, twenty-three-year-old young man,
In shorts, on the ground, on a sunny day.
(I'm forever the art historian,
Grindr a kind of busman's holiday).
Doesn't take him very long to reply:
"Maybe I am"; he says this with a smile.
I ask him how he prefers to be kissed?
"Not too much tongue, it's all about the lips".
Apart from that, we are compatible,
Plus, for this kid, I'd go the extra mile.
He reveals his perineum, his ass,
Doesn't mind if I use my tongue on this.

Another Sext

You cannot find a condom big enough,
You tell me, in the place that you've moved to.
You are not humble-bragging, you tell me.
I admit I have to look that term up.
"Are you, then, exploring being a top?"
You're expanding your versatility.
"I envy literally everyone
Who has had this experience with you".
You then inform me that you feel flattered.
"You remain very dear to me", I say.
You say you flap around, just like a fish.
Still, sex with you remains my dearest wish;
Sober, tender, flailing, or whatever.
You still don't trust? I love you hard or soft.

Antistar

Close my eyes for an old-school dub bass-line,
Then volley my centre of gravity
Between my hips; click together the thumb,
Third finger of my right hand, navel height;
Tense strings ascend in pitch and in volume,
Mudras improvised in stroboscope air;
With my palms cupped together, frame my pate,
"He's really within himself", what friends think;
I'm forming, "I want him deep inside me";
His voice taps on the drum, hammer, anvil,
Stirrup, plays on my auditory nerve.
Rubbish-strewn streets, night bus, bleak dawn walk home,
Massive Attack's paranoid gothic snarl,
The urban in the mode of heroin.

Après Moi, Le Deluge!

I discover I have a fantasy
At the end of my psychotherapy:
That I will be her very last patient,
That she will retire after treating me.
I've very slender evidence for this:
She said she'd gradually be working less.
I understand how grandiose this is,
But also how I can't accept the fact
That it's the right time for us to finish;
When it comes to her love, I diminish.
And yet, sat on the park bench near her place
Was a young man who looked a bit like me.
I assumed he had just started with her;
I am at peace with a little brother.

A Room for Everything

As I am taking myself off to bed,
The cat is washing itself on my quilt,
Central heating on for another hour,
The washing up can wait another day;
A flat pack hope chest on my bedroom floor
Needs someone with a mind that works like that.
I have had my fill of television,
But I am not quite ready for sleep yet;
I want to make time to listen out for
The sound of the rain upon the skylights;
To think about your text from Adelaide;
(Your messages are always a surprise):
"Living with a cat and learning from him,
And I am thinking about you always".

Another One in which Sexuality is Infancy

This guy gives me quite precise instruction
About what he likes; tells me where he's from,
"It's on the outskirts", he then specified,
"Of Sheffield, not in the city centre";
Informs me that he's here on holiday.
Of course he does not offer me his name.
He likes to kiss and works out quite quickly
I enjoy a firm tongue deep in my mouth;
He wants me to be gentle, going down,
Not to use my hand as an addition;
His semen a geyser, then hot lava;
Does not want me to kiss him afterward.
Happy, he doesn't call me a good boy,
But I sense, somehow, I've made a dad proud.

Bad Dancer

Excruciating, the way bad dancers
Solicit their family's attention;
The shame that comes flooding out of each one
As they land heavily and audibly;
As they fail, awkwardly, to pirouette;
As less developed boys struggle to lift.
It is all that I can do not to cry.
In complete control, the lead male actor,
Of each part of his beautiful body.
He is the same kid I saw making out
With his pretty, sweet boyfriend on the train,
Each completely oblivious to their
Homophobic audience, and to me.

Bare-Backing

A guy nearby wants to come in my mouth,
Apologises, fears he's using me,
When I ask if kissing's out the question,
And he politely, but quickly, declines.
I reassure him that I'm an adult,
That, if I wish, I'm able to consent;
That lots of people feel the way he does,
Preserving 'intimacy' for 'romance'.
How to make him understand what I want
In a way that doesn't make me sound nuts?
That, in my sexual orientation,
His ejaculating right down my throat
Is mother's milk, even if that means death?
Better to be fulfilled than not to be.

Bathhouse

A guy in the sauna's biting my lip,
The blood in my mouth tastes just like iron;
Of course, I worry about HIV,
Realise I don't know this young man's name.
I go to the pharmacy the next day,
Buy mouthwash; at home swill repeatedly.
Later, I think of him as a baby,
Wonder if he bit his mother's nipple,
He certainly wanted to cause mine pain:
Pinched them, flicked them and plucked them like harp strings
In a sad song by Joanna Newsom.
What he wanted most, though, was to be kissed;
I concur with him completely in this,
Which worked well: he didn't have good English.

Beard

It's not so much that I have grown a beard,
More like that this beard has grown a Jason.
Now that the hair has begun to soften
And the splintery bristles to lie down,
I'm looking something like a cross between
A tortoiseshell cat and Father Christmas.
The first post-break, group-therapy session
I arrive last, a dramatic entrance,
Immediate centre of attention.
I'm delighted by the things that get said.
One of the men offers grooming advice;
The other notices I'm less afraid.
Who is this grown up sitting amongst them?
What's caused the smile that's lightened up his face?

Bedtime Stories

Whilst I was going to my bed last night,
You sent me a text that didn't arrive,
So I was sad, anxious, and I was sore,
Was filled with my mother's paranoia.
If I had been able, I would have cried,
Instead, I went foetal, and closed my eyes;
A cat on my hip, I turned out the light.
I fell asleep, was out cold for a while.
You've told me how you like to spend this time,
After you've skyped your mama and papa,
You relish being home, alone, quiet.
At meditation, the woman's voice bright,
Like a bedtime story for an adult,
I am surrounded by it, held, silent.

Better Weather

He tells me he doesn't miss the weather,
What he misses is the companionship,
Both intellectual and of [our] friendship.
I reply almost immediately,
Say that there's a Buddhist meditation
In observing the ever-changing sky;
A constant reminder that we're in time.
It is only about ten days later
I remember that I have a rider,
One that took me to Gran Canaria:
I sometimes need predictable sunshine,
A climate supportive of my lifestyle.
I also reach back, notice what you said:
I miss you, still don't want you in my bed.

Birth Order, or the One in which the Group gets
New Members

I was smitten with the first new person,
We quickly felt like we were a couple.
Then, with the following new arrival,
I suspended my former strategy.
No, it didn't even occur to me
To play a relational game with him.
I made room, space so he would feel at home.
The third one raised my sibling rivalry,
But first I was excited that she'd come
And I wanted to make her feel welcome.
It was only when I expressed my need
And she told me she wouldn't rescue me
That I started to unstanchably bleed.
They see: it's part of my recovery.

Birthday Song

"It's not that you have gotten old", he said,
"But that the cold's a bugger on the skin".
It took me six days to really hear Ben
Saying "Happy birthday, I love you still".
A present from Victoria, meanwhile,
On which I rest my head after lights out:
The scent of geranium hand lotion
Somehow helping me to feel less anxious
That if I fall asleep I won't wake up:
I might stop breathing thanks to this illness –
Sleep apnoea I share with my brother.
"It is not for the faint hearted", said James,
"Growing older"; good job I have my friends
To dredge me up to the water's surface.

Black Sun

I can recognize myself in your son,
The way in which he is most comfortable
Not with people, but a fellow mammal;
The way that the world feels manageable
When it is most familiar to him,
When what will happen is predictable,
When the quotidian routines are known.
I remember you, too, as a young man,
Your commitment to fair, firm discipline;
The shame that's attached to letting you down;
How each time that I disappointed you,
By treating, with brutality, a peer,
I'd be polar, you at the equator
And an impossible distance between.

Blue (for Mike)

I'm still not brave enough to watch the film,
Finding that I'm a reader, once again,
I read the script, and think of his garden,
That grey day we all went to Dungeness.
I would sooner lose my hearing than sight,
But what's the scenario where I'll chose?
I found that the most terrifying thought
Was no longer being able to read;
Not the stick of needles making me bleed,
The very idea of which made Eve faint.
To no longer be able to see sky,
Or the slow blinking eyes of my cat's face,
To no longer be held in Eve's sentence,
Is the definition of loneliness.

Breast Feeding

I have been thinking about sucking sweets,
What kind of baby we each must have been;
How, in the back seat of our parents' car,
The three of us would find ourselves fighting;
We'd be offered a sweet to placate us,
Always boiled, sometimes mint, and sometimes fruit,
If we'd been very naughty, liquorice;
Which one of us would first commence crunching?
Briefly, there would be excitement and peace,
Even rarer still, there would be silence,
Which, in our house, meant the radio on.
I'd rarely get beyond a single song,
I'd crack through and swallow mine quickly down,
Regardless of if there were any more.

Butt Plug Pacifier

I immediately know what she means
When she compares, to a pacifier,
A butt plug. It isn't just that both are
An insertive, rubber technology
Disguised to stimulate and to comfort,
Or that sexuality's infancy
Everywhere, for everyone, all the time.
I think back to the months I used mine most,
Never with a partner, always alone,
In the weeks after the break up with him;
The way I would relax, then clench it in,
Consoling myself in the place he was,
The relationship a consolation
For any amount of previous loss.

Chew

I am incontrovertibly better,
It's time for me to reduce my sessions.
I've experimented, I can now see,
"Not able" to attend, repeatedly;
Next week the last time I will thrice see her.
We are both confident it's the right thing,
Can see how much I have grown on my own;
There is not much of a nagging something
At the back of my mind. I can return
If things once again go from bad to worse,
From a rock to an acutely hard place.
Our hope is that it will give me more space
To chew things over in my mouth and brain,
That it will somehow, at last, slow time down.

Chicago Fire

Doesn't everyone experience this?
The anxiety, when you leave a room
That something's smouldering quietly there,
Just biding its time before it then flares,
Flames and consumes everything in its way;
As you cross a threshold, everything gone?
For Victoria, this is not the case;
My little symptom certainly explains
Why the firemen show preoccupies me,
Its characters flat, its dialogue lame;
That said, I cannot get enough of it.
We've talked about object consistency,
Could my anxiety be more obvious?
How often must I have been left alone?

Child/Adult/Parent

When I got back home from group therapy
Last night, I saw someone in the mirror
I recognized: a boy who looked like me,
At my boarding school, aged around thirteen.
This kid had a sweet, open, trusting face
And a big heart, beating with so much need.
His skin was positively luminous.
Didn't have a clue what was coming next.
Not yet defined by sexual history,
By decades of his mother's depression,
Clueless about his dad's adultery,
Nor yet ravaged by his own ambition.
"Trust me, and I will make your life less sore;
I will give you a different outcome."

Claws

I feared that the pain would last forever;
I was afraid she would not forgive me;
Would be easier to let it fester,
But I don't want it to get any worse.
Neither of us likes going to the vets,
The taxi ride, the stress and the expense,
And so I decide to do it at home.
It doesn't work the first time that I try,
The scissors crack the claw but it won't break,
I have not held you hard enough in place.
It snaps, at the painful second attempt,
Filled with dried blood it lies upon the bed.
"How could you do this to me?" your eyes say,
Then you forget, recognise me again.

Circum-Atlantic

Will is putting the rim back into the
Circum-Atlantic rim; Mark is wearing
An ass-free wrestling costume; as for me,
I'm trying a harness for the first time.
At an archaeological strata
So deep you would not know that it was there
From the dirt-free volcanic surfaces,
My inner top's suddenly emerging.
Still I don't get the Spaniard's attention,
He only thinks about where he comes from,
And the group dynamic requires that I
Am the one who cannot get what he wants.
(Of course, I am amidst my two brothers:
Their sexual success and my queer failure).

Circum-Polar World

Will says it's probably sinusitis,
I'm relieved to have a diagnosis.
It certainly makes sense of the symptoms:
Runny and then seriously blocked nose,
The aching pain behind both my cheekbones,
The rolling migraines I have suffered from.
I felt it coming on, on the flight home,
Never guessed it would last as long as this.
Somehow, since I got back from holiday,
I haven't had the energy to shave,
A sign that I had given up on things.
However, on looking in the mirror,
I increasingly liked what I there saw:
Bearded face of a polar explorer.

Days of Open Hand

"From Days of Open Hand to The Hold Tight":
I'll unpack my Facebook status for you.
Before going to therapy these days,
I try to sleep late, have a slow morning,
Eat delicious food and anticipate
The time she and I will spend in the room.
I arrive not full of anyone else.
Toward the end of the Tuesday meeting
Comes the quotidian balancing act
Of remaining in the precious moment,
Of squeezing out every little droplet,
Sticky blood orange juice upon my palm;
And then it's time to say goodbye, let go,
To hold on to the good, without grasping.

Dead Wood

All the tissues I blew my nose into
And the toilet paper I came on to
Make for good kindling under the dead wood;
The fragments used to be a jasmine tree
That got destroyed in a freak hurricane.
I know that I must let you go again,
That friendship's all you have to offer me;
And I remember, strategically,
How bad things were for us those last two years:
The row we had going to the movies,
You spoiling everything that I enjoyed;
How consistently badly I behaved.
Just ash by the end of the afternoon,
Where there'd been so many scented flowers.

Digging in the Dirt

Cuts like a shard of glass in my asshole,
The worst hemorrhoids I have ever had;
I've been forced to take paracetamol,
As well as to continue with ointment;
Maybe an occupational hazard
For people who are passively inclined
But no one has fucked me in the backside
For quite a while; in fact it's genetic,
Something suffered by my brothers and aunt;
I am trying not to feel pathetic,
Using it as a therapeutic goal,
Alive to the sensation of feeling,
Opening myself up to suffering,
Digging in the dirt, discovering hurt.

Don't Go

In my mind, for months now, a scene with Ben,
Maybe at the end of any dinner
Taking place at my house, or maybe the
Very last time that we see each other.
As he is getting up to leave the room,
I say, finally, in my smallest voice:
"Don't go". Mightn't you just stay here with me?
Could we go to sleep spooned like two straight boys?
I am unsure what the outcome would be.
I've rehearsed this sentiment so many
Times, it comes as a genuine surprise
When, today in therapy, I say to
Her the same sentence, and my voice just breaks;
I can see my tears rolling down her cheeks.

Dues

Ten pounds missing from the group payment jar
And suddenly we're live in a new way.
When it comes to blame some members are sure,
They double-checked, it couldn't have been them;
They cross-referenced with one another.
I am not confident it wasn't me,
No way to know if it was unconscious,
And I love what it is making happen,
The defensiveness and the frustration,
Some try to rescue the situation;
One of us is not getting what we want,
Everyone's been a little bored of late;
We resolve: each pay as much as we choose;
I decide to put in the full amount.

Dusk on Rose Street

The sun has gone down; the heating comes on.
In my thirties, I would have been colder,
But kindness now looks over my shoulder
Even as my life gets more monastic.
The purpose is not to be ascetic,
But to know myself in my time alone;
To ascertain, from moment to moment,
What it is that I actually want.
For the last three decades, masturbation
The sum total of my self-relation,
But, these days, without the charismatic,
Beloved man upon the horizon,
I focus instead on the setting sun,
Conscious, each day, that time is running on.

Envoi

Saturday night: the shame of being home,
But the cat is with me; I'm not alone.
It gives me the chance to think about rhyme:
My mixed feelings about sonnet couplets;
Find I'm drawn towards poetic triplet:
My two brothers and I, or my parents…
Enjambment breaks things apart for couples,
To find each other, sooner or later;
Loneliness of the insistent sentence
That won't be interrupted: such bad form.
I'm coming to the end of my tether
When it comes to this poetic genre;
See the last poem as adultery,
A sign that I might finally be free.

"Falling in Love" at the Tai Chi Class

There's something about this man I can't stand:
It's as if nothing bad ever happened
To him, he's so fatuously cheerful;
And friendly! He's the one to welcome me!
How much envy can I find deep inside?
Me, so nervous the moment I arrived;
Me and my Durer-etched melancholy.
Him: experienced adept; me: newbie.
But, a few weeks in, I'm right behind him,
When the entire class pivots on one heel.
(I thud, can barely keep myself upright).
With real elegance, he places his foot;
His elbow poised like a sculpted mudra;
He turns his wrist like a ballerina.

Feed a Cold

The rule is feed a cold, starve a fever,
But it's quite hard to tell the difference:
Whether to lay down, give the pain its due,
Open up, soften around, feel it through,
Or whether it's infinitely better
To stop being a victim or martyr,
To find something more productive to do?
The act of living well takes confidence,
That everything, even the past will pass,
That time's not always something to suffer.
But sometimes it is hard to remember
That there will be, someday, better weather,
That we will keep growing up together,
Rather than me alone, getting older.

Feeling the Feelings

Don't know how to bear this pain in my chest,
A burning feeling of powerlessness,
The rising tides of panic might drown me,
My heart aches, throat constricts, abdomen sinks.
"Take me home": what I want to say to him.
"Don't leave me": what I need to say to her.
She is taking a vacation instead.
He's introduced someone else to his bed.
I work at feeling happy for my friend.
I try to feel content with what I've got.
I can't stop crying in a restaurant.
Manage my affect? Get a little drunk.
The coincidence of these two again?
Losing either a forbidding refrain.

First Last Word

It appears that we have come full circle
And I wanted to give you the last word:
Emily Carr show for our curtain call.
It has been seven years since we first met,
And, trust, I haven't stopped loving you yet,
Now that there's less in the way of my heart,
Less ignorance, depression, fear; all told,
My eyes have clarity, so has my mind;
I've woken up, am glad to be alive;
Still like the cold when it's snowing outside,
But prefer, these days, to be safe inside,
Laid in the bath, snowflakes on the skylight:
I don't need to write another sonnet,
And I am nowhere near done breathing yet.

Floating World

A continent all vulnerable coast,
Whose interior's hard to inhabit,
Has developed an amphibious boat,
"Designed to capture cities" is the boast.
Me, the product of an island nation,
I see that I am in competition;
There, subtle, conversational battles,
In which he is determined he will win.
He tells me that, as a child, it took years,
To put his head fully under water.
Up to my neck, I like nothing better;
And I'm fully confident I can swim;
The quiet world revealed through goggles,
Suggests who is kicking and who's floating.

Fluffer (2)

He wants to find a way to include me
In the conversation, his excitement.
He selects an academic excuse:
"Object-oriented ontologies".
Invited to admire their idiom,
To join in, before the interruption.
Today, I tell him, he seems much brighter;
He informs me he is feeling worn out,
Both from his contact lens experiment
And from spending last night with his new beau.
Then he drifts out of the conversation.
The timing was, once again, quite telling:
The three hours spent messaging each other
Led to their first sleepover: a fluffer.

Footnote

"With my shoes off, it feels more intimate".
She doesn't miss a beat: "It's less adult".
And that is now what I'm supposed to want.
Plus, the session's ending early today,
As I'm on my way to give a lecture.
Eve's on my mind for so many reasons,
In that period between her birthday
And the anniversary of her death:
With her shrink, feet resting on their footstool.
It's light at night, the tulips coming out,
Summer term; the passing of the seasons.
One bardo on another this April,
Each with its opportunity for grief
Then possibility for a fresh start.

Four Scenes of Detachment

Growing up, my father would go away,
To a related military base,
Sometimes for days, sometimes for weeks or months.
These were referred to as his "detachments".
Mum must have felt sustainedly afraid
My philandering dad would again stray.
Back at home, we'd stay up late with my mum,
To try to help her feel less lonely.
Betsy asks me why I use "quite", "indeed",
Senses pain in these forms of agreement.
Jealous of Ben's erotic escapades,
I wince inside, try hard not to spoil them.
Like Ani Difranco studying stones,
I no longer want to feel so at home.

Fresh Start

To have found a therapist at forty,
And to not have metastatic cancer;
To be listened to, always, patiently,
And to be challenged so consistently,
Is helping me to finally slow down,
And to realise this experience,
Its qualities, are what my life will be.
He may not have picked me as his boyfriend
And, worse still, he has chosen someone else;
She may have left me for her new girlfriend,
And ceased to understand why this hurts me;
But I'm not dead, an opportunity
To find something now better than them both:
A group, a shrink who gives me what I need.

Frost, at Midnight

The cuneiform script upon the snow
Suggests this winter, circum-Polar scene
Isn't under-populated at all.
In fact, it's a haven for a poet.
Take these rural woodlands, for example:
Here, the queer hoof-marks of a famous horse,
Whose rider tugged at the bridle, to pause.
These are the footprints of Iris Dement
Walking, some, with Anna Akhmatova;
Russian writer, American singer.
He won't see me; is not at his window.
Loneliness led me to this palimpsest;
Each of these sonnets a consolation:
In poetry, no-one's quite so alone.

Full Fathom Five

2009: York Art Gallery
Is exhibiting Sashiko costumes
From Japan: ghostlike, hanging cruciform,
Without their heads, hands, calves, feet, or forearms.
That said, there's no sense of extremity,
Only peaceful rectilinear forms
That recall a hugging body, the sea;
Not only because worn by fishermen,
Because patches of fading indigo
Conjure up a dark marine horizon.
They've themselves undergone transformation:
Lacking the grandeur of a kimono,
Each patch was a swatch of former garments,
Each swathe, like a sonnet in this sequence.

Gay Mini Break

How did it take me so long to know this?
When I see so clearly my vengefulness?
In the Easter break, you went to Berlin,
I am about to leave for Las Palmas,
For my own classic gay sex holiday.
You replied, when I told you about this,
"I cannot imagine anything worse".
But, last week, you wished that you could be there,
Whether to be alongside, or with me,
I find myself genuinely unclear.
I wish that we were going together,
In a relationship closed or open;
That I could watch you swimming in the pool
Because you've never looked more beautiful.

Generosity, in the Tai Chi Class

The man I want shows up in fewer clothes,
And I just want to be stood close to him;
More than that, to be adjacent, naked.
I am getting better, a few weeks in,
At least at manual calligraphy,
If not overall choreography.
I'm beginning to understand the form,
What is below: the ideography.
Richard suggests: "don't give too much away",
In a forward-pushing, repulsive mode,
In order to retain integrity;
You could have guessed how much this spoke to me.
The move I love best: picking up a thread
To heart-height, drawing it across my chest.

Going Home

Do I imagine this scenario?
Or does my shrink watch me through her window
As I leave her garden, depart her street?
I imagine her hurrying to see
Me from the space of her consulting room,
Over the last weeks. As I walk away,
I have to keep myself upon my feet,
Feel myself limping inadvertently.
I discover that my left knee goes numb
And that my right elbow hangs awkwardly;
Scars from two of my attempts at self-harm.
I do my best to try to keep going,
Look out for the handsome cats watching me;
Smile, weakly, and blink back at them, slowly.

Greed

My greed got the better of me again,
Should know by now that this has a pattern:
If it takes him a week to be open,
He will shut back down the following day.
Plus, what was I hoping for anyway,
In this endless game of hide and go seek?
That he'd finally write up on Facebook
"People, what did I do to deserve him?"
So I, with genuine grace, could reply,
"I'm not really sure that it works that way".
I try to persuade all my friends to see
That the best view of the world is spotty,
Through the middle ranges of agency.
Light another incense cone. Start again.

Group

How've I not written, until now, about
The group? Not spotted the resemblance
Between poems in this second sequence
Which are more individuated, but
Related, and my Wednesday ritual
Of going to a Quaker meeting house
To talk through things in an open circle?
Partly, I've been respecting privacy,
Long waiting on an appropriate form
To capture this novel experience.
But, two and a half years later, I find
The form's been under my nose all along:
In book two, I don't have to be so strong,
I describe a group, and not a couple.

Hannibal (for Angus)

Imagine me, if you will, Will Graham,
In the television show *Hannibal*.
(Were you expecting William Shakespeare?
My identification's still more queer).
What is at stake in my feeling, like Will,
More or less in love with a cannibal?
At some point in the show, someone asks him
If he will survive the relationship.
He answers that he's not sure that he will.
Here's where I saw the spider in the cup:
To love someone who'll kill every person
And then consume them for his own pleasure,
A person who may just kill you as well.
How often I've returned to rev this up.

Harm is in Us (for Sara Salih)

Like a hawk, I spot rabbits from the train.
Once I've seen one move, I detect the rest,
Rooted to the ground, like a live soft toy;
In their fearful faces, one profiled eye.
Immobilized in a laboratory,
In some barbaric 'cosmetic' eye test,
The tearful, fellow rabbits look depressed.
What brings these frightened creatures into view?
The compassion of an abandoned boy,
Left sobbing as his parents drove away?
The indifference of one driving by,
Thinking "not my responsibility"?
I stopped drinking milk, all of a sudden:
A vegetarian's not a vegan.

Harness

I honestly don't know how she does it,
Since what she asks me: "Is that a new shirt?"
I smile in recognition; "not really".
"It feels like you're somehow in your upper
Body differently"; doesn't miss a beat.
I haven't yet said about the harness:
The way it made me feel oddly secure,
The sense of having, at last, some power.
The beard was probably a giveaway,
Suggesting my new masculinity.
"I think you're telling me you're in charge here".
I immediately feel quite nervous.
She sees, beams: "I'm not going anywhere";
I feel easier in our power share.

History

In last night's dream, I get to the exam,
And it involves a choice of book reviews,
Where I don't recognize a single thing.
Somehow, I realize where I've gone wrong:
The price to pay for not attending class.
Only, normally, it's Biology,
In this reoccurring nocturnal scene,
Whereas, today, A Level History.
Mostly, I want to run out of the room,
But I think: what's the worse that can happen?
I will spend a year doing it again.
It's clear this has to do with therapy,
That I'm not ready for my last session
One-on-one, but I won't be left alone.

Hope Chest

"It takes thirty minutes to assemble"…
Five days later and I'm still struggling:
It's true that some things in life just take time.
I need my brother or Victoria
If I'm ever to put this together.
I got pretty far, right up to the lid,
But the later drawings just don't make sense!
So it sits, unfinished, in my bedroom.
At my shrink's, I must have walked up the stairs
At least 200 times without seeing
The hope chest resting upon her landing,
It's almost exactly the same as mine.
She's said, so often, you want to live here,
I can see now that she knew all along.

He Sends Me Pictures in Underwear (for Craig)

James recommends a book I didn't know,
On learning that I'm reading Dickinson:
The Gorgeous Nothings is by Jen Bervin,
Marta Werner, and also Susan Howe.
On page two-hundred-and-twenty-seven
An "Index of Envelopes by Page Shape".
The eleven, off-white, hand-written flaps
A laid-out drawer of once-designer briefs,
Like the ones worn by my new (would-be) beau,
Who first came on to me a week ago.
What can this super-cute man see in me?
I want him so much it makes my heart hurt.
He proffers so many kinds of relief,
I feel reborn, in a landscape of hope.

Horizon Line (for Hal)

Hal's got me looking at horizon lines,
Orienting myself towards distance;
Glancing up into the air, at the clouds.
The Storm Cloud of the Nineteenth Century
Once again calls out, from its shelf, to me:
Ruskin's meditation on the green sky.
Constable's aerial microcosms,
The only pictures, at Tate, I could see,
Suspended, mid-air, in cumulus frames.
I sit in my attic long afternoons,
Thinking Victorian geology,
But find myself looking through the window
As water condenses, shapes, and deforms;
At every moment the sky is changing,
And, like one long asleep, I'm awaking.

Horizontal

Outside, the snow blows by, horizontal,
Past the Habit's second story window.
Inside, you're feeling cold for the first time.
We both keep folding our cuffs up and down.
Appetising your fair, hairy forearms,
Your strong fingers, thumbs, and extended palms.
You take off your glasses, put them back on,
Bow your head, look at me over their rims.
Neither of us seem to want to go home,
Mid "such a productive conversation".
You're praising the cross-generational,
Tom Ford's film of Isherwood's Single Man,
The beauty that you find in the Koran.
Your hug, full of love, it crushes my spine.

Hot and Bothered

"Not up for fun" is what his profile says,
But his image tells a different story:
His legs open, sat in his underwear,
His face looking straight at the camera;
Showing off his ink. Kneeling on the floor
Is how he has positioned the viewer,
Close enough so you'd know his aroma.
"You have got me hot under the collar"
I write to him, from a shopping centre,
Where I'm sat on a bench after dinner,
Browsing the library of local gays,
Grindr's most proximate ecology.
He laughs aloud: "I'm a total poser,
And it was a hot night in Headingley".

Hourglass

I'm up to my ankles at Scarborough,
Salt on my lips as I am breathing in;
Sun behind my head, in the universe,
Casting a shadow across the water;
Incoming tide changes my silhouette,
The sand bank dissolves beneath my cold feet,
The saline grains exfoliate my skin.
The film that I am taking of this scene,
Wobbly, low quality, from my phone, an
Obvious metaphor for identity,
Grasps a superficial geology;
Deep inside the earth's crust, the molten core.
I'm some from home, but glad to be alone,
Right now, I relish the complexity.

How to Bring Up Your Boys Gay

Giving kids' assholes loving attention
At the heart of being a good parent;
Peristalsis represents working through,
Excretion when something's not good for you;
Teach cleaning yourself up when you are done,
Washing your hands so you can start again.
Encourage children in masturbation,
So as to enrich their self-relation,
Explain that this is not a shameful scene;
Better, provide a spacious, private room.
Be relaxed at each cross-generation,
Older and younger your inspiration;
I'm being, of course, metaphorical,
Also, perhaps, absurdly literal.

If It Makes You Happy

Remember the last time that we were here?
How late you were; a queue for the shower;
I wonder who you were with to this day,
Who was in your bed, who was frowsing late.
Looking back, I feel humiliated,
Giving you those poems, birthday presents,
Worried that you didn't have your glasses.
But, today, I woke up early to a
Black cat, grey morning, a mint green leaf tea,
Feeling warm and mellow, bright as yellow,
Hopeful that I'll get to hang out with you.
"Eat slow", Izzy says. You text "EXCELLENT"
When she cancels and I confirm our date.
The lengths it goes to make you happy, Fate.

I'm Not Alright, You're Not Alright

Everyone looks at me with bafflement,
When I say I don't understand the phrase
"I'm alright, you're alright"; a stock in trade
In our transactional analysis.
So one of the men explains it to me.
It's as if fireworks go off in my head.
My relationships just don't take this route:
I either feel anxious or arrogant;
Relieved that I'm not the one feeling worse;
Someone doing better makes me afraid;
A sense of equilibrium if we
Find ourselves doing equally badly.
Sexual competition is most acute.
It all comes down to sibling rivalry.

Interior Decorator

How many times have I seen these pictures
As I have walked up and down my shrink's stairs?
I have breezed past, without noticing it,
Probably hundreds of times, this mirror.
I haven't given them a single thought
Until now, this our last July session,
When, suddenly, the sequence makes good sense:
On the landing: a sunset or sunrise;
Climbing up the flight: anticipation;
Going down again, her patients descend;
At the bottom, where I put on my shoes,
A chance to see my reflection once more,
Endless water-colour waves on the shore,
My shrink watching from the window up there.

Internalised

I've been thinking about the sonnet form
And its relation to my therapy;
How I am less concerned with the rhyme scheme
As long as I can get the right line length.
The ten-syllable rule was containing
As a psychoanalytic session.
The sonnet sequence like weekly meeting,
The recto Tuesday, the verso Thursday.
The left hand page her, the right hand page me.
Sexless couples the traditional theme.
Rectangular shape: analytic frame.
Relational silence: all that white space.
I'm looking at you from every leaf.
In reading me, you are holding my gaze.

"It's Betsy's child, whom I last saw – life passes /
In a mirage of claims and counterclaims"

And so in our penultimate session,
Back to my being vegetarian.
She can only see it as a weapon
I use on the human population
To gain the moral high ground, upper hand;
Keep myself special, make myself different.
I point out her disavowed aggression,
The real murderousness of eating meat.
She then retorts: "I don't care what you eat,
It's what you do with it that concerns me".
We have waited three years to have this fight,
And now there's agreement or there is flight.
I thought we would finish differently:
On days like this, I can't wait to be free.

Jacob and the Angel

Ben's writing to me from Australia,
Tells me of his version of The Dreaming.
He conveys two scenes in particular:
He's wrestling a kangaroo in one,
The second focuses on sheep slaughter.
Both allegories of his relation
To his country's political culture.
Which one of these won the fight, I wonder?
When I try to choose, I'm honestly torn,
Deciding the one that I admire more.
Jacob and the angel, I remember,
A scene that describes wrestling and fucking.
A world in which there's so much suffering,
To which, on balance, I'd still be reborn.

Japanese Paper Flowers (For Izzy)

It's been so long since we sat together,
But reading about Proust brings you to mind:
His "Japanese paper flowers tightly
Folded, that blossom and develop in
Water" involuntarily take me
Back to then-frequent Sundays at Goji,
Where we would order some sweet Osmanthus,
With Bakewell, as a matter of routine.
Even then, we felt how precious it was,
Not to mention how very lesbian:
To watch the bud un-ball as a flower,
Nature's own female ejaculation.
Then, one day, a sudden interruption.
We're still, here, beyond metamorphosis.

Jase at 43

In mid life, my body is filling out
With what? Masculinity, I suppose.
I am thinking of starting my own press,
I have ceased to believe in peer review
Which just comes down to some people like you
And others don't. Hold on, did I say "just"?
Some readers have scorched my writing to dust,
Have splashed on paraffin, set me alight:
I am sick of being a burning monk.
In my shoes, what did Joni Mitchell say?
"What's romantic love, but a kind of joke?"
Kate Bush was asked for her favourite singer?
Replied, immediately, "the blackbird".
I am not sure I could have agreed more.

Karma

A sparrow lies dead on the bedroom floor;
This explains all that purring in the night,
The kind after drinking running water:
Low, erotic, and deeply satisfied.
I'd forgotten how light bird bodies are,
Light as flight, air, as a pile of feathers.
I shrouded it, in tissue, in my hand,
Carried it outside like a ring bearer,
Lowered it into the bin, closed the lid.
I saw the bird that I thought was it mate
The next day, perched on a telegraph wire;
The cat looked at me; I looked at the cat;
I thought a little on cause and effect,
Hard to escape interwoven karma.

Koromogae

Ending is all that we can talk about:
There are five sessions left, then we are done.
(Only, of course, I'll keep going to group).
I can see that her eyes sometimes tear up,
Though, in myself, I cannot find sadness.
There's certainly disavowal my end,
Also it's clear she has done a good job
That I don't feel this as abandonment.
For me, it is more like koromogae,
Indeed, this fall, even the timing's right:
A seasonal ritual when people
First box up one brood of their kimonos
And then unpack an alternative set
For the remaining six months of the year.

Last Session

The last session before the Easter break,
A bitterly cold day on Micklegate.
It seems that I don't want to let her go;
Remain awake is all that I can do;
My bowels have become hot, liquid and loose;
I cannot seem to keep my body warm;
I don't want to be alone anymore;
What my body does now that she's leaving,
Introduce a time-lag in my thinking.
She praises me for opening my heart,
For bursting into tears in the session;
I am talking slower, feeling closer;
Our feet extend out towards each other;
Curled up in her lap, like she's my mother.

Letting Go

The scaffolding goes up on next door's house:
She's having her roof completely replaced.
For a few weeks, at least, I'll lose the space
Of the attic as my most private place.
On each face, there's a large picture window,
Through which the tilers will cast their shadow.
The timing may be helpful; I'll let go
Of the hold I have on myself, for now;
Will sit and my desk and be virtuous;
Will save, for my bed, my superfluous
Desire, whose return is continuous;
A quotidian ritual of waste;
The joys of living alone in my house,
Unshamefaced, usually, without a spouse.

Life Support (for Mary Baines Campbell)

I have spent these last weeks reading sonnets
By Rafael Campo that my friend Kate
Put me onto, having read about him
In an interview, in a magazine.
It turns out that he knows my friend Mary
And Eve Kosofsky Sedgwick, both poets
That I adore, and both muses of mine.
I find his forms, whilst my shrink is away,
Containing, holding, like a life support;
Calm whilst I am within his idiom.
The medical poems to me deeply
Revealed my new preoccupying themes:
Death, nothingness, illness, complexity,
The man I loved twelve thousand miles from me.

Line Breaks

Another way to think of this morning:
The moment that he sees I'm on Facebook,
He is excited that I am awake,
And unselfconsciously reaches for me.
Then it's my fault that there's an hour's delay,
As I make black tea and have my breakfast.
By the time that I see I've been addressed,
He's railing – about Westminster Abbey –
To his father, and our moment has passed.
There was so much that I wanted to share,
Having been storing things up for a day,
About James Merrill's Prose of Departure,
What he and Eve are doing with line breaks:
The gaps between them so full of fearing.

Madeleine

"Madeleine cakes are sometimes called 'cat's paws",
So Carol Mavor's *Black and Blue* informs,
And I find I'm profoundly reassured
To be, myself, in such good company.
Before now, a sense of perversity
In my inhalations of feline feet:
The queer olfactory pleasure I gained,
Undercut with sodomitical shame.
The soft, gorilla-like black of the pad;
The scent of cat-litter and of the path;
An ear bent with a saliva-laden
'Hand'; luxuriously extended claws.
My pet has grown thin, her miaow quiet,
This I shall miss the most after her death.

Matins

Closing her book, I find myself wanting
God himself as a reader: grandiose.
Desiring his attention, but unsure
What it is that I want to say, to ask?
Joni Mitchell found herself furious,
Whilst Louise Gluck isn't faintly abashed.
"I can't tell you how much I loved watching
That corkscrew of gulls yesterday at dusk
Riding, hugger-mugger, on a reverse
Helter-skelter spiral of rising air;"
Or "I'm so angry you leave me like this.
Why must you keep yourself so separate?
You can't be completely self-sufficient.
Maybe you've nothing of interest to say?"
Still I reach for you, the start of each day.

Migraine (after Dory Previn)

I am ready to let it go, some days,
Vengefully; this life that I'm tethered to.
Can't you stop the ride? I want to get off.
I'm feeling nauseous, like I might throw up;
My skull's cracked right open, with a migraine,
Extant meds don't work for this kind of pain.
It feels like it's been this way forever,
That there never will be better weather.
Then I think of the vow I made my cat,
That day I got chosen in the shelter;
This creature needs feeding, requires water,
I am this patch of darkness's carer;
On the train, two boys with moon silver skin;
Ok, alright, god damn it, deal me in.

More Bad Karma

We cannot stop punishing each other,
I don't turn up to your birthday concert,
You cannot come to our Sunday brunch date.
Yet we're also kind to one another:
You tell me you wished I was in the hall,
That, whilst singing, you wished to have felt me;
I reply that I am truly sorry
To be determined by our history,
That I hope, some day, things will be different.
We're both stuck in the drama triangle:
Victim, persecutor, and rescuer.
Ben and I broke free of our bad karma:
When I think of him now, he's over me,
I'm coming under his kind, warm body.

More Lessons from the Tai Chi Class

Earlier in his life, Richard tells us,
He used to be a ceramic artist.
Now he works in mental health services
And, on a Tuesday night, teaches tai chi.
I can see he'd be good with his patients:
He's thoughtful, flexible, relational.
When we're playing with the form of wu-chi:
"It's like holding in your hands a vessel".
For a moment he's lost in reverie;
Or, he's offering us pedagogy:
"But the difference between pottery
And this - here there's no object permanence".
Getting my body to move more slowly,
Without leaving a trace: just right for me.

My Father Returns From the United States

My little brother tells me that my dad
Is going to move back to his home town.
He has lived near me for the last decade,
And we've been out of touch, at my bequest.
But still I find that I feel abandoned.
I cannot see why he won't fight for me.
I've been remembering when, as a kid,
After some months, he returned home to us
From detachment, from the Royal Air Force.
These days I fear that time in Las Vegas
Almost certainly meant adultery,
If not whores. He came back radiantly;
From then on, never used a knife again;
The glamour of his non-conformity.

New Year's Day

Izzy is in pain and seeking ritual.
I suggest maybe burning a candle,
Making new light and warmth, letting wax go;
Or going to feed geese on the river,
Scattering stale bread upon the water,
Giving scarce resources to the wild fowl.
But I catch myself trying to fix things,
Wonder if I'm unable to bear her
Pain, if she also can't tolerate it.
How hard it is for both of us to sit
With her little girl left out in the snow
Not always taken in by a neighbour.
May this be a place to let yourself sing?
Relating hold some of the suffering?

On a New New Horizons' Photo of Pluto (for Nicole)

This photo of Pluto's a Rorschach test:
The Bering Straight across a frozen sea;
The spread of an ice-age, newly forecast;
The tail of a white whale, obviously;
Milky marble in a childhood pocket,
Worn down, part smooth, part pocked to the finger,
Circles within circles upon this sphere;
An image of object in/constancy,
Still out there in space, this sometime planet,
With new clarity, it can now appear,
Here, in its eccentric, inclined orbit;
The facture of coffee, thick latte paint;
A dark inside a white chocolate sweet,
Of the kind I would, by the handful, eat.

Open Relationship

"What's happening's never what you assume",
Mark cautions me kindly; it's good counsel.
And later that evening, he kisses me.
His husband's my best friend; he is nearby.
It all started in this bar in Berlin,
Ben is in a back room, with a stranger;
Our relationship doesn't recover.
I feel torn apart, rather than open.
Then there's this maddening paranoia,
Finding its climax in the thought of him,
Making out with that sidekick of a girl,
In spite of how much I love his body.
Behind all this, watching my mother see
My father's constant infidelity.

Opposite

You move round the table, sit opposite,
Remembering that my back likes support.
Now we can easily make eye contact.
You tell me about a drunken night out,
The two friends that you took to the Habit,
Both flirting with three nearby teenage boys;
How they followed you all from there to Dusk,
How one of the boys kept kissing your chest.
Next morning, displaying your confidence,
Insisting there was nothing wrong with this.
Appearing sophisticated these days
Means staying open to adolescence.
I wince at your sexual incontinence;
Still missionary in our abstinence.

Ozymandias

What might Eve have said? "It's hard to credit",
"The turbulence it brings", "one single step
Over the line", into that "kid picture":
The "pipeline back" to 70's Malta.
Seeing my brothers and I sitting there,
The comforting texture of the sofa,
My handsome big brother's arms are folded,
My baby brother looking radiant.
And me, determined to be separate,
Maybe, already, in some way, apart,
In spite of Mike's pinkie upon my hip;
What has already happened to that child?
Mocked by his dad out of his speech defect,
Been told he is fat, and that fat is bad.

Paradox

In South Germany, thirty years later,
I'm swimming with your kids in the water,
A substitute father when you're not there;
I'm throwing up, into the sunny air,
Your cautious son and more robust daughter.
You tell me that you don't believe in pain,
Or illness. I quickly recognize this
As the cause of my decades-long distance.
I sulked, I clung to our former closeness
'Til my shrink said "get over it, will you?
It was literally tens of years ago".
I felt so betrayed, and that it was fair.
Something shifts; and I can have it again:
The heartfelt tenderness of your embrace.

Paratactic

Andy really wants me to suck him off,
And then to shoot a week's load down my throat.
The same time, he's nervous of meeting up,
And asks me to film myself jerking off.
This, in turn, fills me with anxiety;
Now I'm probably as afraid as him.
Each of us trapped within our little moat,
Whilst genuinely wanting to hook up.
Of course, I will be the one to give in,
Once, with his cock in hand, he facetimes me.
His brief, deep voice gives me firm instruction:
"Take off your underwear, and then stand there".
The irony is he's just up my street,
And this is the closest we'll get to meet.

Patchwork Quilt

Truth be told, I can't even remember
The last time I put on this quilt cover;
The cut jumped up, quickly started padding,
Sensing a new chance for self-curating;
The pattern has gone quite out of fashion
But it is one that I chose for myself,
Not one my ex-boyfriend chose for himself;
I can see I have to give his bedding
To charity, my shrink wasn't kidding.
Things will get easier in my own skin,
Waiting patiently there my kith and kin
And Izzy has come back to me at last,
Because I was less afraid of my wants,
I have given myself a second chance.

Peri-Performative (London)

I had so wanted to show them London,
More precisely, my mastery of it;
Provincial boy who'd been born in Lincoln,
Keen to show them how well he knew the tube.
It was crowded and Eve didn't feel well,
Then there was the impenetrable heat:
(The clichéd Imagist descent to Hell).
Hal took control of the situation:
At the bottom of the escalator
He put his hand firmly on my shoulder,
Told me we were going to take a cab.
The right thing to do, we could afford it.
At Sloane Square, we had Holy Trinity
To see; my shameful asininity.

Phone Sex

I must be a little delirious
On the long journey back from Las Palmas,
A cold coming on, jet lag setting in,
As I think Davey's the taxi driver.
Do you remember him from last summer?
The man with whom I had all that phone sex?
Who Victoria called "Mr. Brit porn"?
It seems he's warm and friendly in person.
I send him a message when I get home,
Asking if our paths have possibly crossed?
"That's not what I do", he says angrily;
Then remembers me erotically;
A text arrives ninety minutes later:
I've heard him come, now I see the picture.

Poem for Ivor

"People cannot marry ice creams", he said,
"But men can marry men; women, women".
He also described to his father how
"In the olden days, this was not the case".
Stuart and I are sat by the Minster,
He is barefoot, in shorts, and a t-shirt,
I am tickling his son, who loves it,
His fearless daughter plays at a distance.
I ask if it will make a difference,
To how his children understand gender?
He thinks, that there will be less foreclosure.
Thirty years ago, we're sat in the snow,
Both on the cusp of becoming young men,
I love him as much now as I did then.

Portrait Miniature (For Tom)

How gentle this connection between us;
How quickly trust has opened up my chest;
How my heart is heavy with his sweetness;
A little uncertain of my success;
How much I only want to talk to him
In a room full of my colleagues and friends,
Red-threaded together, a kind suture,
Even facing away from each other;
How, almost immediately, I want
To know what kind of underwear he wears;
The kind of idiom in which he writes:
A prose poem, a portrait miniature,
A language of desire, quite like mine;
Hunger, to have my skin across his skin.

Postings (for Tamsin)

On the walk home from the office today,
I decided to turn my music off,
I needed to spend some time with myself:
Everything felt grey, the air was damp, cold,
But then I heard my favourite singer:
A starling; and then I saw another:
A blackbird; a spring-green pussy willow;
A cat made eye contact through a window;
A funny dog better than any text;
A world populated with so much life.
For the past few months, since you came to stay,
I can't stop thinking about what you said:
"There is nothing upon the internet
More interesting than what's in your head".

Preterition, or, 'The Day Before You Came'

I have thought about this song for so long,
Mostly, what is it that might transpire
In the missing period that is left,
The time the words leave unaccounted for?
We know, for sure, it takes our heroine
Three quarters of an hour to get from home
To work, and that she leaves at five each day.
We meet her, much later, at her front door,
Asian food in hand, at just about eight.
There's no mention of timetable delay
Or long queues at the Chinese takeaway.
What does she do that can't be mentioned here?
What, in her day, is so unspeakable?
Suicidal thoughts or something sexual?

Protest Song

I was meant to be in a seminar,
To be making a grant application,
But if the head of my institution
Can't support the views of the union,
He doesn't get my good will, my weekends;
And I'll tell you the truth: I just don't care.
I would prefer to watch the sun go down,
With the cat, from the comfort of my room;
Stand at the mailbox in the golden hour,
Sending love to my nephews on postcards.
Colour me Mary-Chapin Carpenter
In pajamas, for spiritual reasons;
Let's drink to the end of vice chancellors,
Take back our hearts, minds, our avocations.

Queer and Bookish (For Angus)

What is this book that you hold in your hands?
Its gilt spine is bound to last a lifetime,
Like a butt crack its pages are open,
Black starfish words quiver under finger,
Which an expertly placed tongue might dilate;
The musty scent of dusty old paper,
The scratchy, quite intimate cursive crawl
Of someone else's marginalia;
Laid on a table, sitting on your knees,
Maybe, between men, read adjacently;
Surrounded from behind, in someone's arms,
Maternal, homosocial, and sexual,
A queer and bookish scene of reading, and
An upturned child's face, pleading, "look at me".

Queer and Now

"You know what he's like, he's just being gay",
Over the backyard wall, my neighbor says;
Exasperated, repeats it again.
Sound travels through this row of terraces,
So, of course, I hear it as I'm reading.
"We are no longer a minority"
Is what I had claimed only yesterday,
"Now that even gay marriage is legal".
Makes me regret throwing back her son's ball,
When it came over the fence once again;
Makes me glad that they'd have heard us fucking;
Makes me wish that I'd have come louder still.
How many times I've been kind to her face;
When he hit her, me who called the police.

Recovery

I've been thinking about recovery.
In therapy, on Tuesday, my shrink said
"When it comes to your personality,
I think it all comes down to injury;
Physical as well as emotional".
This was apropos of my desire
To, perhaps, learn a peaceful martial art.
She asked me if I would be please be careful
Since my skin already hurt and my heart,
And since I'm once again falling downstairs.
It maybe safer to be more restful.
So, this afternoon, I lay on my bed,
With the new book by Mary Oliver;
An autumn sun in a dramatic sky.

Re-Enactment

We are lying on your bed together,
The first night after you move to London,
And, of course, you cannot turn off Grindr.
Four year later, how much pain I am in.
The bath is where I make the connection:
The cat cannot be close enough to me,
The last night at home of the holiday,
The dread of return to that fucking school.
I feel nauseous, alone, sad, powerless:
This is entirely beyond my control.
Helpless, I must have channeled my father,
Understand he couldn't bear to leave us,
Because of the way it made me so brusque,
In our coffin, a thirty-year-old nail.

Same Situation

A gap of two days and he's back in touch.
He describes "konking out" on Friday night.
I make a joke: "anxious attachment, much?"
He replies, says, "that is partly my fault".
Then I make light of the situation,
"This dates back to well before you were born".
But it's true his comings and goings hurt.
Why can't he just end a conversation?
Though these days there's less interpretation;
In his mind, he's not finished with me yet,
There's continuous object relation,
He picks up my breadcrumbs where they were left;
This space between us again and again,
Why can't I see the bun's in my oven?

Sanctuary

Two cats have now moved in with my mother,
Leaving behind their other, proper homes.
When owners came looking for one of them,
She let their calls come in through the window;
The cat raised its ears, but kept lying there.
Today, the second cat is giving birth.
My mum noticed the lowered abdomen,
The movement of kittens within its girth.
She sounded so peaceful; happy again
To be in her maternal element.
After an hour, I started to wonder
If I was as magnetised as each cat:
The promise of a world bent to my needs,
Of gourmet food when it came to my feeds.

Sapokanikan (for Joanna Newsom)

Joanna walks down a Manhattan street,
Past a fire engine with tears in her eyes,
Sings of monuments buried under snow,
Of boy soldiers sent to the Western front;
There are trumpets and there's a recorder.
And I watch, with tears streaming down my face,
I have the song on a looping repeat.
In the future, there is still a hunter.
If, at forty-four, I am still alone,
At mid-life, there is still a way to go.
Finally, we come to the last session,
It is everything I want it to be.
I reach the door, look back, and don't despair,
I am confident she'll remember me.

Satori

My shrink is taking her June vacation;
Before she leaves, I set myself a task:
My project is to enjoy waking up;
Early morning's are when I feel most lost.
On the Tuesday morning, it's 10.04,
What's normally the start of our session;
Today, making notes on *The Way of Zen*.
How've I not seen this relation before
Between Satori and my ambition?
My shrink gave me a helpful instruction:
Told me not to reach, first thing, for my phone;
"What is X doing?" I am not to ask,
Til I have poured some tea into my cup,
Have felt my way into my emotion.

Scott of the Arctic

In February 1984,
The snow fell three feet deep upon the ground,
The fog was so thick you couldn't see far,
But, like ship's masts, the rugby posts floated.
I went out to catch hyperthermia,
To die, in the frozen Arctic tundra,
The first day of that thirty-year winter.
Decades later, the bergs began to melt.
At first, nothing stranger than dew on pelt,
Then polar bears got disoriented,
Defensive, to try to feel less frightened.
When there was no place left for them to hide,
They gave up hope, swam out to sea, and died,
In the brine where the whales became extinct.

Sculpture Victorious, or Queer Little Gods

At the festival, Vibhuti tells me,
Statues of the Hindu god Ganesha
Are brought offerings, are dressed with garlands.
Then some time passes and it's all over,
And the whole household walks to the ocean.
The majority of the family
Stand huddled together upon the sands,
Whilst someone, presumably the father,
Walks, into the sea with the elephant;
And, at some unspecifiable point,
Just lets go. Waves take the part-human god
Out, deeper and deeper, through salt water.
There is nothing he can do except drown.
The family go home: the empty shrine.

Self-Portrait with Pupae

Behind the glass, a Joseph Cornell box:
At various stages, eighteen pupae
Suspended from five blue sticks whose colour
Ranges from indigo through to turquoise.
Ten cases, crumpled and brown, like old leaves,
Hang, upside down, like vampires, in the eves;
Five ranged, a spectrum from lemon to green,
Byzantine-saint gold, the remaining three.
Each contains a micro silk-factory.
If you look at the surface of the glass,
By contrast, you get a portrait of me,
My face largely obscured behind my phone,
My left hand is raised as if I could bless.
Listen: echoes of Herbert's 'Elixir'.

Sibling Rivalry

Sexual jealousy makes me seem friendly
But, in fact, turns me mean. Just when it seems
That I am being complimentary,
I'm making you so anxious it's obscene.
It's true I am telling you a story
In which you appear to be the centre:
We're talking James Merrill, Australia,
It feels like a metonymy for you,
But you pinpoint the heart of the matter,
Asking if we referred to you by name?
My first thought that it is one and the same,
Yet you're half a world away from the room.
I need to bring this out in the open,
Own the extent of my competition.

Sixth to Last Session (July 21 2015)

Back on this day in 1969,
You walked upon the surface of the moon
For the first time. It must have been sublime
To have a view so far away from home,
Scary to not know if you could return;
And not a sound out there but your breathing.
The disorienting pause at each line's
End, the prominent static filling in
The small gaps between each word and sentence.
You still had to flag your territory,
Even as you moved towards being free.
To feel both weighted down and weightlessness,
The gravity-less pull of the silence
Of deep space; first anchor-, then rudder-less.

Skin Feeling

Where do these ideas for poems come from?
I'm reading about Henry Protheroe,
Beached up on his bed, outside his swaddling.
Waking, in my new quilt, the first morning -
A stripy texture, cyanotype blue -
The cat "sleeping" next to me, ears alert.
Hmmm; is the first transitional object
The sensation of textiles on "one's" skin?
Is this why, today, I love brushed cotton?
The comforting feel of adjacent felt?
A Pliocene memory from the cot?
The pajamas he left me when he went -
My ex-partner - I tore, put in the bin,
No longer his boy, I must be adult.

Smoothing Things Over

Today, she's at her most transactional,
Doesn't want to express an opinion,
Regarding whether it's historical,
Or an attempt to turn up the volume;
That, or to solicit her attention.
"So, tell me what am I supposed to do
With this never-ending anxiety?"
She gets me talking about my weekend:
I describe digging up the hardened soil,
Sitting on the ground, breaking it by hand,
Then brushing the earth into a fine tilth.
She really likes the part of the story,
Where I'm unearthing shards of pottery.
She says, "Keep spending time in your garden".

Snapsh

Somehow this image helps me to feel safe;
Perhaps better, it's keeping me afloat:
I am in my wet suit in the water,
It's later summer, maybe mid-October;
The sky is grey, the ocean's also grey;
I am bobbing there, looking out to sea.
The photograph may be in black and white,
Or that's just the character of the day.
Someone's on the beach, I'm not by myself,
There's a person there to take this snapshot.
The cold salt water soothes my burning heart,
The saline scouring more pain from my life;
I can't touch the ground, I'm out of my depth,
The tide, though, tugging me back to the shore.

Snapshot

I found a book of photographs online,
Full of images taken of the moon
Published in the year before I was born;
My interest in the photographer
Of lunar portraits – full page, monochrome –
As viewed from a satellite orbiter,
The fact they were by my friend Eve's father,
Whose depictions of his poet daughter
Recur throughout her various poems:
In violent, momentary flashes,
Looming above, from behind his camera,
He takes her photo, also more from her:
The brilliant light of Hiroshima
Reducing his young daughter to ashes.

Sounds True

"When you have finished eating, wash your bowl".
Like so many of the things that she said,
It sounded Buddhist, it seemed so simple,
Yet it took me more than three years to learn.
It is hard taking care in the present,
Not getting in the hangover habit.
Of course, it takes time and isn't much fun.
Then, I started looking forward to it,
Found it's sustained work, but not unpleasant:
With less to fall over, more time to choose
Which expensive bowl you're going to use,
Which, of the many you have, suits your mood?
One of the ways to be a survivor
Is to chop up wood and carry water.

Spring Break

I've left emotionally before the break,
I can feel myself disassociate.
Right now I like to be in bed by eight,
A nightmare where I shout myself awake.
A holiday booked for the day after.
"The more you miss me, the more you will have".
"Not missing me is just self-destructive".
"If you are feeling desperate, then don't".
"Don't prod it to see if it's still alive".
"Work as hard as you can at living well".
"Try not to feel like you don't give a damn".
"Try not to grasp at what's not meant for you".
"Your fantasy's a world away from you".
"Take time to digest, rest, reflect, review".

Steam Room

The sound of water dripping on the floor;
He sits opposite me in the steam room,
Playing with his cock beneath his towel;
How to signal that I'm available?
I extend my toes in his direction,
Open my legs, fondle my erection,
Looking him straight in the eye all the time.
I decide I will go sit next to him
Rest my knee against his; my skin, his skin;
He kisses with his tongue outside his mouth;
I pinch, caress the tip of his nipple.
He's not English, I ask him where he's from,
I nearly laugh aloud when he tells me;
Fate smiles, flirts, delays: "Gran Canaria".

Still (for Gina)

"The problem with Gothic cathedrals is
That they are always under construction",
Gina writes from her European tour.
I have worked so hard to protect myself,
Yet still I am not invulnerable:
I had put your boyfriend far from my mind,
I had hidden you from my Facebook wall,
But still I learn he's coming for Easter.
Must I destroy you to defend myself?
Say you don't know how to have a good time?
Better to admit that I'm envious;
To realise that it's not either/or.
If I fall down, I must get up again;
Pick up my chisels, return to the stone.

Still Life with Pears (for Victoria)

What was Victoria trying to say
To me, with her ripe pear allegory?
About eating them at the right moment;
Equal danger in their being unripe
And being altogether too tender.
Something to do with not being alone
Or grieving too long, and a reminder,
Of not trying to move on too quickly.
I must let the plaster on my walls dry
Before I try to decorate again.
My shrink defined my personality
As containing serious injury.
I cried, seeing the bare brick walls that night:
Their wounded structural integrity.

Still Life with Anamorphic Skull

Growing older, I want to change my name
From Jason Edwards to Jason Sowter:
I have had no contact with my father
Since the fight when he came out from prison,
My family on his side full of poison;
The final straw: the scene with my cousin
In the park: as if the threat were Dylan,
The boy who's brought to me nothing but joy.
In addition, I find I'm growing bald,
Like my uncles upon my mother's side;
I'm sobered by the sight in the mirror
Though I'd wanted thinner hair all my life.
The gap between my teeth from my mother,
Her dentition, my vision of the grave.

Strange Attractors (for Peter)

Susan warns against misapplications
Of key phrases with technical meanings
From the sciences of complexity;
Yet the poetic possibility
Proves almost impossible to resist.
For example, first there's "strange attractors",
Those unpredictable perturbations
That yank you from orbit into transit;
Then there are "uncertainty relations",
Patterns of "convergence" and "emergence";
At the edge of this universe, "chaos";
The project of "de- and re-coupling"
In a dynamic homeostasis.
How could I not gravitate towards this?

Stranger by the Lake

In my dreams I go down by the water;
In my writing, there are many drowned men;
The Shawn Colvin song tells of her daughter;
The death drive of desire, in the film.
After forty minutes on my summer,
She asks: "what is it that you still won't say?"
It's not that what I've said so far's not true,
But she can tell it's not the whole story.
I thought of sex with someone HIV,
Whose picture I had admired on Grindr;
Hearing how he wants after the murder,
She notes, "just how angry you are with me".
Funny, I hadn't made the connection.
Queerly, I go down to the lake alone.

Summer, 2014

Imagine this poem written for Eve.
A patchwork quilt of leaves and of petals,
Embroider me a kimono in silk,
With hundreds of midnight-purple flowers,
A constellation of lobelia
Starred and freckled against a slate-grey ground;
Alternatively, speckle the fabric
A palette of geranium colours,
Or with a facture of hydrangea;
Unfurling, like prehistoric fern leaves,
The flashing lining hosta-green and gold;
Or, still in the idiom of Merrill,
Dot, with darting house martins, the loose cuffs,
Dashing to and from their nests in the eaves.

Tales of the Avunculate

I scour the world looking for your two sons,
They feel like my centre of gravity,
Wherever they are, then there is beauty.
Around them I feel literal hunger:
To make eye contact, have conversations;
Better still to kick a football around.
So different from playing with my brothers,
These boys don't know that I don't do team sports,
That, truth be told, I'm not really a boy,
That I'm not confident in the outdoors,
That I'm not comfortable in my body.
Victoria said, when she met Dylan,
"He's constantly looking, beaming at you;
Couldn't love any more his Uncle J".

Taxi Ride

The taxi driver wants to talk to me
The whole way home about his game of golf,
The course he prefers, how it's exercise
Without all the tedium of the gym.
There are so many lessons for the self:
Visualising before driving off;
Imagining putting as adventure,
Relaxing, no concern for the outcome.
He says that his game's got ever better,
And, after an hour of group therapy,
I identify with his sentences;
His journey's quicker and less expensive.
Near the end, we talk about the weather:
How miraculous the spring always is.

Telegraph Cable

"It's raining in London", Fiona says,
When I tell her I'm sat in my back yard,
Reading Eve's poetry, that "it's heaven".
Her report makes me again realize
That I am inclined to idealise.
Ben cannot always be in the sunshine;
Come on, Jason, if it is summer here,
And he's Australian, it's winter there;
Just as when we write to one another,
My early morning's his late afternoon.
So when I feel his attention slacken,
The rope lose all its tension from his end,
He's not necessarily with his boy,
He may not have anything much to say.

That Poem About Rimming

It's been on my mind again, his asshole.
Before I met him, there was not a man
Alive who I would have thought of rimming,
Though I came close with Max, who waited, still.
Like everyone in my generation,
My first experience of seeing this,
Was, perhaps, witnessing Stuart, Nathan,
In their Manchester loft conversion bed.
I also feel the need to acknowledge
A certain riverside, apartment scene,
Where two lesbians found they weren't alone
In having wanted this kiss all along.
This morning, the thought of his puckered folds
Made waxy, wet with my lubricant tongue.

"the aura of this / fantasy world. Warm. Golden. /
Intoxicating."

Angus and I are discussing fishing,
As a predatory activity
And as a retreat from the outside world.
The larger context: how to deal with pain
And fear, in the plotline of our loved one
As seduced by our other beloved.
Then something characteristic occurs:
This most gentle man is suddenly whorled:
He imagines water enveloping
The overalls of the man in question,
"The moving, differential pressure of
The impersonal, warm hands of water",
I note. (For the sake of full disclosure,
I've added the word "warm" so it will scan).

The Book of Ephraim, Redux

After our long text exchange at midday,
I'm reading Eve's essay on Ephraim.
She is touched by "the strength of the spirit's
Attraction" toward the two mediums;
"The fitfulness of their interest in him".
I'm quickly deflated with poignancy,
Remembering our earlier friendship:
How random your boredom and interest.
I was fully in the willow-ware cup,
You had your mind on your latest pick up.
These days, it's ok that we disagree
About my favourite show on TV:
You find nothing to like in Hannibal,
But, in common, we've still got James Merrill.

The Castaway

Another way to think of this series,
Is to think of individuation.
In group, a bit, over the last few weeks,
Someone has called me on my use of "us".
Of course, I'd always followed Eve in this,
Her love of the dear, first person plural:
We; Oui, the French affirmative for "yes";
(Also "wee", a word for urination).
Un-lonely me, and anybody else.
The person I mentioned didn't agree;
Did not like to be included this way;
Did not want to be in one of my cliques.
Each poem first born, then swimming alone,
Too briefly held in the inter-crural.

The Depressive Position

I can see that, when I end therapy,
It won't be euphoria that I'll feel.
But I also won't be devastated.
My feelings, they will be profoundly mixed.
Being ambivalent is not much fun,
But it's safe, relationally stable.
At least there is not the endless volley
Of the paranoid schizoid position.
Instead, more like a series of tossed coins,
Where, each time, you land, it's predictable,
Plus good enough quite a lot of the time;
And, if you wanted head, but got a tail,
You pause, pick up the coin, and flip again,
No upped ante, no teleology.

The Discovery of Mother Voidness (for Victoria)

The Discovery of Mother Voidness,
The words of Jankya Rolway Dorje
Adapted from the Thurman Translation,
Edited to autobiography:
"I was like a child who'd lost his mother,
Couldn't find her, though she was always there;
I would think 'yes, yes, finally it's her',
Then catch myself, 'no, no, it's someone else';
Or 'could it be, really?' another day;
Various, different subjects and objects,
All examples of the maternal face;
These births and deaths and metamorphoses
All repetitions of her changing place.
"Liberation's still possible": his claim.

The Freshness of Slow Learners

A new goal for the end of therapy,
But how I've come to loathe this tai chi class;
How much I have hated it from the start:
The discomfort of being my body,
In front of a mirror, in company;
Of being worse than everybody else.
Even though I've only been there three times,
And there were things that I liked, even then:
Every single action wasn't inept;
I liked the way he said it was private,
That we should each feel alone in the room;
That we could feel free to play with the form;
Then, those moments of synchronicity,
Were, every time, like cat-nip to me.

"the hours-long bouts of sexual reverie"

Eve describes masturbating for hours
As a child, a way of staying alive;
Of providing for herself a stable
Environment, warm and self-attentive.
I have gradually comes to terms with this,
When it comes to my own experience;
That it may not be pathological,
Necessarily a downward spiral;
That it's also not just a waste of time.
That afternoon, I skimmed through all twenty
"Cum, cum, cum and more cum" compilations,
Seeking home amongst the repetitions:
The man licking cum off his partner's thumb,
The one image that I squirrelled away.

The Leftovers (Beware Spoilers)

What to do when you lose something you want:
Give up your family and profession?
Smoke cigarettes with the guilty remnant?
Wear a white uniform out in the cold?
On a school bus, detonate a grenade?
Find your faith in an Old Testament God?
See that coincidences still happen?
Try to believe it's all part of a plan?
Go down to the river and don't come back?
Kill off, inside yourself, the hurting part?
While you wait for it to feel different,
Listen to post-minimalist music?
Stop hoping for the person to return?
The writer offers no explanation.

The One in which the Poet Doesn't Want to be in Therapy
Anymore, Again

Not remotely what I thought would happen,
When presenting my need at therapy:
My shrink found herself feeling impatient;
Someone in the group told me to fuck off.
But I guess that I learned a life lesson:
Asking the least available person
For help is really looking for trouble;
Seeking to be rescued as an adult,
Is inappropriate, however hurt
Your vulnerable, inner infant might be.
So what am I to do to help this boy?
Don't want to tell him "enough is enough";
I want him to get his needs at last met.
I give him comfort: we sit, with the cat.

The One in which the Poet Embraces, At Last, His Masculinity

I leave Will behind on the upper dunes
(Whilst I am gone he will fall fast asleep,
Unafraid of getting burned or cancer),
I long to be in the tidal water,
Love being in the company of men,
Watching and smiling at one another,
All in the salt-water-world together;
A pretty Asian man's closest to me,
The handsome man from yesterday wades in,
I bruise both elbows and I cut my knees,
But in the healing waves nothing matters,
Unusually buoyant is my body,
Not boyish, but muscular and manly.

The One in which the Poet is Woken Up Early on a Saturday

Week days, I'm woken up by the alarm
Which isn't waking up in my own time.
The cat doesn't recognize the weekend,
Scratching to be fed at seven a.m.
So I stumble to the bathroom to pee,
Then go downstairs, put some food in her bowls:
Crunch, crunch. I wait for the kettle to boil
And go back to bed with two cups of tea.
The sun rose, gold burnished the aerial;
A corvid waddled across the roof tiles;
The cat focused, cackled, went back to sleep.
This, why Mary Oliver wakes early:
The neighbourhood quiet for nearly two hours,
Each breath a pause in which the world appears.

The Number Six, to Osbaldwick

There's a bus that leaves the end of my street
And takes you all the way to your old house;
Except that it takes me, rather than you,
And you don't live there any more these days.
Plus, I never ride the bus, because it
Is just as fast to walk, as wait on one.
I thought about this coming home last night,
Then saw the umbilical connection.
Me tied to you, more than the other way;
Before, the uterine environment.
They want me to stop sleeping on your sheet
And to throw away your old pajamas.
First, need to find an alternate to this
Still mostly hard-to-resist regression.

"The Real Elements of Heldness on a Day-to-Day Basis"

Waking up with the cat, in my own time;
A masturbatory self-relation,
Then urination and defacation.
Being able to take a bath alone.
Through Facebook, feeling in touch with my friends;
Boiling the kettle every few hours;
Seeing things growing in my back garden;
A writing project in media res.
In the cat box, pan-handling cat shit;
Tidying up stray papers as I go;
A continuing drama on tv;
The sense of sexual possibility.
Making prolonged eye contact with the cat.
Remembering to breathe in and breathe out.

The Warm Decembers

Along the bleak fen road to his home town,
He is driving us back from Great Yarmouth;
The pain's so bad that I nearly break down.
Though not sure he'll return to the hotel,
I'm relieved; freed from the car's constrained hell.
Earlier on, he takes a photograph
Of my hand, in close up, on the table.
Years before, Eve's Beatrix is in the bath,
She's also brutalized by her father,
Grows up into a fat photographer,
Escapes the Norfolk seaside boarding house,
Develops a U.T.I., heading south.
How much less lonely had I, then, known, dear,
You'd researched your narrative poem here.

This Writing Assignment is So Gay

On Wednesdays I go to group therapy,
It turns out there's a homophobic guy
Who otherwise seems to like me, but who
"Just doesn't want to have to look at it".
Nobody else says "this isn't ok";
At this moment I've never felt more gay.
I find myself inclined to challenge him:
"Do you come across men fucking often?
Did you receive a gay porn subscription
As a birthday gift you could return?
Because in the world we both inhabit
Queer people are scared to even hold hands".
I am totally sick of this bullshit,
Please can I have another assignment?

Title Poem

Only four more days until she comes back.
How much decongestant can a man take?
How much insane migraine medication?
These: take two, but only once every day,
And the packet warns against addiction.
I find I cannot breathe since she's been gone,
And that my head hurts all the fucking time;
Can't remember time without nausea,
Or what it's like to have an appetite.
Will I get over my abandonment?
Or will it floor me intermittently
Until the last day I finally die?
My three themes: nothing, death, complexity.
Good choices and autobiography.

Tom at the Farm (for Ben and Emelia)

Going there, like going into the past,
To a place where my heart's desire was,
To the family of my beloved,
Who died long ago, yet somehow remains.
It's pitch dark, driving through the Black Forest,
Suddenly in the road are sibling deer,
Disoriented by the headlight's glare.
A hawk arcs in, takes a sparrow, full speed.
Of course, there's always murder in the air,
Farms seem like concentration camps these days,
Hidden in plain sight, miles out of town,
Where each irreplaceable animal,
Has a life first foreshortened, nature morte,
Then terminated, the whole thing routine.

Toothbrush

I went to buy myself a new toothbrush
And, when I got home, I discovered that,
After three years of using the old one,
I'd brought myself an exact replica.
Until that moment, I couldn't have said
What the first one looked like in any way,
What my criteria were in choosing,
What the new one's defining features were.
An allegory of my desire:
It's typological consistency;
How much is down to my unconsciousness.
Yet in my mouth how different it felt,
How alive, strange my teeth were in brushing,
How happy I felt when the job was done.

Tough Call

Say I wanted to speak to mum or dad
From my boarding school, once grace was finished
I'd run, at break-neck speed, down the dark hall
To the one telephone available.
It helped if you were seated near the door,
If you were a superlative runner,
And, with all things there, if you were older.
If lucky, you'd have time before roll call,
To pick up the receiver, feel hopeful.
After the change in tone, dial the number.
Dinner at home would be over by then,
The painful scene of my parents, Michael,
With them, the two cats, Tigger and Suki.
A tough call: loneliness, or poignancy?

Two Texts About Fisting

It's only on the flight back to Stansted,
I realise that I've received not one,
But two, separate texts about fisting,
One each from my significant others.
Can't tell if I'm being complemented,
By appearing thus in their fantasy,
Or if they are both competing with me?
(Of course, it might just be coincidence).
In answer to one, "I haven't yet been";
"Greetings from Gran Canaria" is my
Answer to the other. Reality
Is more prosaic, characteristic:
Still searching, amidst all of these gay men
For one, with a mother's welcoming face.

Umbrella

To open it up took me quite some time,
Didn't know there was a button to push,
But then your umbrella sprang right open.
This is a fine, kind souvenir of you:
The way it looms above me, like you do,
Wants to protect me from the wind and rain,
Presses on my stomach, into my palm.
It offers me the opportunity,
To think through holding your hand in Paris;
Still I find I'm afraid of losing it,
Want to keep it for myself, in my house,
Not let anyone else steal it away.
Half a world apart and still in my heart,
Something like object constancy at last.

Wake Up!

When she was tired, how disturbing it was,
And how much I wanted to wake her up.
How abandoned I felt with him asleep,
As if he were withholding or angry.
When anyone's quiet why can't I feel peace
And take some interest in my own thoughts?
Can't I feel solitary in company?
All these poems, why can't I let you be?
I'm still craving more object constancy,
When I read Eve on object permanence.
This came after the helpful difference
Between her engagement anxiety
And her subsequent attachment issues.
Each idea's a new metamorphosis.

Well Hung

Yes, it's really called a commando strip,
However much like a vaginal wax
It may happen to sound when said aloud.
For months I've deferred putting the print up,
Worried that I'd do something wrong somehow,
Even if I followed the instructions,
That the walls themselves would come tumbling down,
I'd inadvertently destroy my home,
Trigger a scene of parental shouting.
Izzy, of course, hit the nail on the head,
When I said "I keep checking they're breathing"
(As I did with Dyl when babysitting),
"It's not that they are anxiously attached,
Nudge them and see; it's that you are Jason".

Words, Last

"Is Sufjan Stevens gay or Christian?"
Someone asks; an interesting question.
It's similarly hard to read the tone
Of our weekend together, in Brooklyn.
The final scene is him sat at the gate,
Reading, waiting for me to board the plane.
The flight moved forward, I was nearly late.
How he suffered on the subway through Queens.
It's the confined space, the lack of consent,
And the unpredictable impingements
That conjure, for him, his violent dad.
I say: "I'm hurting because you are hurt".
I was feeling anxious, a little sad,
At Marcy Avenue, but also glad.

YMCA, or, Reality and Realisation

It's hard to imagine how no one knew,
Watching the Village People video
For Y.M.C.A., that they were not gay.
The cop, the construction worker, cowboy,
The native American, army guy,
The muscle-Mary handlebar porn-stache,
The ursine body hair, the black leather!
And yet, this is what happened on Tuesday.
Richard asked how we should end, at Tai Chi:
With something serious or something fun?
Tired of learning, I opt for the latter.
Much later, some way into the sequence,
What we have been doing, I realize,
Is YMCA, but in slow motion.

You Can Stop Now

Three years ago, I began this sequence;
Rather, I commenced '1441',
Never dreaming another would begin.
The first poems were a kind of monstrance,
To a man I loved, who is now a friend.
The subjects of these are more various,
And so the question comes: of how to end.
Each time that I did not know what to do
In therapy, my shrink would say to me,
As if it's the simplest thing in the world:
"Don't do anything". (A hard one to learn).
In *A Dialogue on Love*, at the end,
Eve hears Shannon say that she can stop now.
For myself, I've still no idea how.

IV

The Ballad of Tam Lin

The Ballad of Tam Lin

"What kind of curse is this?" I didn't ask,
As you, in my arms, became a brown bear,
With a baritone growl, rough, thick, dark hair,
Whilst I, scratched by briars, lay securely there.

"What kind of curse is this?" I didn't ask,
As you, on my chest, became a lion,
Your torso muscular, hirsute, and tan,
Gelled up into a 'thirties quiff, your mane.

"What kind of curse is this?" I didn't ask,
As you, in my hand, became scolding iron,
That stung, like an oven burn, on my skin,
Yet still, you could hear the drop of a pin.

"What kind of curse is this?" I didn't ask,
As you, in my mouth, became a hot coal,
I savoured the taste, then swallowed you whole,
Through scorched oesophagus, I'd reach my goal.

"What kind of curse is this?" I didn't ask,
As you became a naked man at last,
Unaware of the metamorphoses
You had undergone in gaining this bliss.

32074816R00104

Printed in Great Britain
by Amazon